MAKE EVERY DAY A WINSDAY

MIND-SHIFT | METHODS | MASTERY

DERRICK BUTTS

Ordering Information

Quantity Sales – Special discounts are available in quantity purchases by corporations, associations, and/or networking groups. For details, contact Derrick Butts at the e-mail address listed above.

Individual Sales – Contact Derrick Butts at 972-895-2WIN or www.assistu2wincoaching.com.

"Everything rises and falls on Leadership."

John Maxwell

The 21 Indispensable Qualities of a Leader

TABLE OF CONTENTS

PART 3: MASTERY MAKEOVER

Dedication

This book is dedicated to every bad decision, disappointment, failure, and pit that I have ever experienced. Also, I am grateful to my professors who didn't kick me out of their courses, and I know that each of their classes helped me to develop my purpose.

Even if I don't always like the path I had to take to get to this moment, as I get older and wiser, I have learned to recognize how this path held the necessary steps for my growth and character. I continue to learn to let life take its course. I have not always been this way.

In the past, I've been guilty of judging a book by a chapter, and one's life by a season. Maybe you have too? The harm in this approach is that you can celebrate the wrong people and miss out on some real heroes. I ask for forgiveness from all of those who have been hurt as a result of my choices and decisions, and please know it is my earnest desire for you all to make every day a Winsday.

MAKE EVERY DAY A WINSDAY

To my parents, brother, and sister, I love you. To Tamara, Sariyah, Torin, and Zion thank you for sharing me with my Assist U2 Win clients as we are all building this business together. To my investors, Joe Sanders and Stephan Cooper, thank you for believing in my dream from day one, and financially providing me with the seed money to start. Lastly, to Smokie, our dog, who sat by me in the early mornings and the late nights, making sure I didn't work alone, your company became soothing even though I don't like dogs.

Introduction

I was on a cruise with my family. Everyone was having a great time, and all I could think about was the life I dreaded having to return to, and live in, in order to keep the smile on their faces. I knew in my gut I was supposed to be doing something different, something bigger, but I felt stuck in what I had to do.

Some of you reading this book may also feel perpetually stuck. Maybe you feel trapped in your career, and you want a better job, a different job, or you may want to leave your job. Perhaps you have the job you want, but feel stuck in a relationship, and need a win in a relationship. You could be tired of sitting home on the weekends, wishing you had someone to enjoy life with, or you may want to enjoy life again with your spouse or mate. No matter what attracted you to this book, I want you to know the content was written to confront any areas of mediocrity, procrastination, or settling that may exist within your life. I said any, which means you may have to do some soul searching to find the exact place where you are stuck, but once it's identified, it can be confronted. **Eighty-five percent of the things that have changed in my life first had to be *confronted*.** When we avoid these areas, we are giving them permission to remain. The longer anything remains, the stronger it becomes.

As you read through my stories, I want you to think about your journey. I often say every "aha" moment carries the seed of possibility for breakthrough and transformation. **An "aha" moment is when some word/sentence jumps off the page and speaks directly to you in your particular time and circumstance. Upon hearing it/reading it, you claim this idea, and activate it into your present difficult situation. Being willing to activate your "aha's," means looking for that seed of possibility that you didn't know existed before. Once you recognize your "aha," claim and activate it, then you become more open to receiving and activating the next "aha." Activation can become a habit. Activating the "aha" is the first step to winning.**

You will soon learn that there's a difference between having a lot of followers (likes and shares) and having a true tribe (accountability and growth). I surrendered the title and switched lanes when I became intentional about my reason for being online. I want to disrupt one's day, life, and plans. I call this "Intentional Intersections." I want my Facebook Live, e-mail, text message, or direct message to intersect with someone's excuse, emotional meltdown, frustrated attempt, and inability to concentrate. When the message of winning meets this individual, the opportunity to decide arrives. That decision begins with this question: **What am I going to do with knowing I don't have to stay here, feeling like this, remaining stuck, or sitting idle another day, unless I choose to do so?**

Settle in your heart and soul—right here, right now—that before you have a mindset, you will make a mind-SHIFT. If your mind has been set, and it's set wrong, then what? If your mind has been set that you are not smart enough, cute enough, qualified enough—or whatever enough—then you will surrender your seed of possibility and hold on to your sentence of reality.

I challenge you to make a mind-SHIFT. Mind-SHIFTS travel to new locations and scout out the land. Mind-SHIFTS decide that their "not yet" is better than their "right now." Mind-SHIFTS get a glimpse of their future self and begin making decisions with their present self in order to make that introduction possible—sooner rather than later. You can't become what you can't see or imagine. It's this kind of thinking that will find a way to go to work, and still find the strength to write their book, work on that business proposal, apply for those high-profile jobs, and even go back to school, and prepare for their *next*. Mind-SHIFT individuals get up earlier, stay up later, work smarter and harder, get up after failure, and still figure it out while smiling, so you don't know what's really going on with them or in their lives. **Mind-SHIFT forces winners to win within before they ever win without.**

You see, until you've had a mind-SHIFT, you don't need new innovative methods. Methods should be saved for those who are going to do something with them. Don't get me wrong; comfortable coasting people can still learn these methods and have little gains. Oh! But I didn't write this book for incremental growth only. I wrote this for those who desire a quantum leap. Yes, for those individuals who are tired of cycled living—New Year's Resolutions, then Valentine's dates, to Spring Break, to a visit at the hottest church for Easter Sunday. Let's make it two in a row, so you return to service for Mother's Day, and then prepare for summer vacation. Don't forget the 4th of July fireworks, and soon you'll be back-to-school shopping during Tax-Free Weekend. Who's barbequing for Labor Day? What costumes are we buying for Halloween? And, for this year's grand finale, we've added a new item on the Thanksgiving menu, with a little black Friday shopping, and some Christmas gift-giving as the last item on the agenda until we do it all over again on New Year's Eve.

If you're tired from simply reading that, or if this sounds anything like the cycle you live or see, then the methods we're going to learn will free you and help you break the cycle with a new mind-SHIFT. You'll learn methods on time management, productive income activities, and how-to systems on minus to multiply. You will learn how to delete and delegate before you add more to your long list. The methods standalone, but when you combine them, they will yield exponential growth. We end this book by learning how to move from maturity to mastery.

Mastery is experienced when we sprint to the decision line of change and execute with a marathon mentality. **My siblings taught me that mentality.** They both enjoyed their days around track and field. My brother ran cross country, while my sister ran track. For the record, my father beat them both up until his forties, and then he decided to retire. I believe he was undefeated. **His long-term outlasted their short-term.**

Store this next statement, "Long-term consistency always outlasts short-term intensity." Mastery bridges long-term consistency with short-term intensity. Let's go and dive into each of these areas and begin to *Make Every Day a Winsday.*

PART ONE:

MIND-SHIFT OVER
MINDSET

Mind-shift can be defined as challenging all forms of mediocrity to experience new levels of possibility.

Chapter 1

From Mindset to Mind-SHIFT

"Set your attention on your intention."

Mindset means everything. **What if I tell you that you are capable of doing and being way more than you are right now?** Do you immediately embrace the question and begin thinking about what else you can do, or do you immediately start listing all the reasons why you'll never be able to accomplish the results you so desperately desire?

Your mindset determines the side of the coin that you focus on. *Your mindset is the energy, feelings, and belief you use to approach and attack your day.* Some call this your attitude. Others refer to this as your mentality. For us to be on one accord, we are going to use the word mindset. What is your mindset right now? Is your glass half-full or half-empty? **A half-empty mentality becomes the approach we use to look at ourselves, but when we see others, we offer them** a half-full mentality. **Most of the time, how one views one thing is how they'll see everything**.

The law of First Mention is a term I learned in Theology Class, which holds true 98% of the time in life, and that is how something is first introduced to us is generally how it is carried out. Without giving you a Sunday sermon, let's look at this principle when it relates to our mindset.

Those who are positive can usually find positive traits in most of what they encounter. You may have gained weight, and they focus on how it's good to see you today. Positive individuals have a perspective that can be annoying at times. Everything can't have this spin of positivity. Some things that happen to us are just downright not right. The flip side is true, as well. A cynical person can receive something positive and still find a way of seeing the negative in it. I recall a time when I gave someone a $100 bill, and the first response I received was not thank you. It was, "That's not even enough to pay for the entire bill." I thought, *Wow! Let me remember never to give them any assistance again. They see negative even when positive occurs.*

What's rare about the situation I just described is, oftentimes, this law is only broken when it relates to how *I see/perceive* other's situations. This individual believes that greater is available; it's just available for you, and not for me. I realize this more and more as I coach people who believe for others yet can't find that muscle to believe in themselves. Have you ever encouraged someone to jump, and then couldn't get yourself to take a baby step? I've seen some of the most negative individuals give some of the best encouragement. They can make someone else smile, but they walk around with a frown. They can show someone else a solution, but the only thing they talk about when it comes to their life is all their problems.

We all, from time-to-time, are on the giving end, and then there are the times when we're on the receiving end. It's when we're on the receiving end that we need to borrow the mindset from those who are charged and are full of energy and life.

In Texas, we have a store that may not be all over the U.S. It's called *Rent-A-Center*. For those who may not have one nearby, let me explain. A *Rent-A-Center* is where you can rent what you need until you can afford to purchase it. Man, oh, man! I wish there was a Rent-A-Mindset! If only I could unscrew your head and give you a different mindset for the day. This would be both good and bad. When it comes to mindset, I think you'd be okay, but then you'd have a new set of problems. (All I'm saying is, most of the time, who you are is who you are.) **Let me give you an example.**

Over the past year, my travel schedule increased, which has had me in and out of airports and hotels. Growing up, I always desired a job that allowed for travel. Being a military child, we moved residences every three years, and the thought of travel has always been exciting. Okay, secretly, I loved seeing the men and women who wore business attire on a plane. Walking down the aisle headed towards my seat, I would watch them with their laptops and notepads out working on something that had to be important. I was amazed, and my inner voice would say, "One day, that will be me." I always felt they were talented people because they traveled in nice clothes and seemed to focus on doing more than just complaining about if their ticket had them stuck in the middle aisle of a 2-hour flight. (Okay, that is a bummer;

especially, if you're flying alone. Instead of one shot of someone talking to you, now you have two opportunities. Ugh!)

My travel had me going in and out of different time zones. From the West Coast to the East Coast, I would land in different airports and quickly had to adjust. One of the first things I'd do when the plane landed was to check my cell phone and see if the time updated; you know these devices are so smart. It would automatically update the time to the current time zone as soon as the phone received a signal from one of the cellular towers.

As a creature of habit, my phone would update, and the next thing I'd do was take off my watch and manually adjust the time from the time zone where I'd been to the current time zone of where I was. This wasn't a difficult task, but it is vitally important. To keep on track with my calendar demands and appointments, if this wasn't done; everything would be affected because I'd be operating my *now* based on the information of my past. Isn't this why some companies are no longer in existence? We can either adjust and evolve, or we will soon stay the same and become extinct.

Mindsets are similar. There are factors like our experiences, exposure, environment, and education that shape our mindset. We all have something we do today because of something or someone in our past. I speak and pray in a similar style to Scott Wilson. Scott was my youth pastor growing up; he influenced my life across many areas. Today, I am a John Maxwell Certified Coach because of an introduction to the *Injoy Life Club* at an early age. I pray by walking and pacing the floor. Scott did that as well.

Think about who has been that influencer in your life. What qualities did they hold? The influencers of our lives have shaped our current mindset. Now, this can be good and bad. Later in the book, I'll share some juicy details of the bad things I've learned to appreciate from my life, but for now **I want you to understand that just as I had to adjust my watch to match the current time zone manually, so you have the opportunity to do what I would call a mind-SHIFT.**

MAKE EVERY DAY A WINSDAY

As you read this book, you're going to see that everything falls into one of three categories: **Mindset, Methods, or Mastery.** I started with mindset because it's the most important of the three. Our mindset must be monitored minute-by-minute. We must diligently think about what we are thinking about. Why? **Because we often bring about what we're thinking about.**

I challenge you to shift your thinking. No matter where this book finds you, I believe there's a mind-SHIFT for more, and when you adopt it, you will be catapulted into your next level of breakthrough. There's an unlimited level of abundance that is waiting for you. When I said that an appropriate response should've been, "You're right about that." Unfortunately, this level I'm referring to is not experienced because of some limiting belief, known or unknown, which exists around our lives. The layer of our personality that we function from is not the most authentic version possible. It's just the version we choose to accept and present to those around us. I want you to leave that level and begin stretching for the level of abundance that is assigned to your life. This level is available for you and me. I said for you, and there's enough left over for the person you told about the book. There's more—yes, much more—available!

Are you willing to go beyond the limits of comfort? Are you willing to challenge the borders? Are you willing to push past what you know to experience your "don't know yet" possibilities? I don't want you to get to good and stop. Let's trade in good for great. And, for the select few of you who are currently playing at great, there's something called greater for you, too.

This book is intended to stir, stretch, and shoot you into a whole new frequency where the vibrations of winning are tapped into every day. You see, until one has an experience with what they can be, they will never leave who they currently are. You must get a vision of the new in order to leave the places of the old. I see it for you. I can't come in contact with you, and not see the seed in the midst of your dirt. Mindset chooses to focus on either the seeds of success or on the dirt of your failure. I choose to see both as ingredients in my winning formula. That's just one of the ways I "Make Every Day A Winsday."

As we prepare to dive in, please go back to my cell phone and watch experience to glean the most important factor about mindset. My cell phone adjusted automatically, and my watch had to be adjusted manually. Mindset functions the same way. You are wired and bent, specifically one way or the other. You are pessimistic or optimistic, naturally. This is your default. When left up to you, this is how you normally function. Yet, with this information, we must all realize we can change—or shift.

I had the option of letting my watch remain in an old-time zone that was right for where I'd been; it was just wrong for where I currently was. Too many of us are functioning from an old download. There's an update we need to initiate in order for us to experience the full capabilities of our lives. Our mindsets can have a mind-SHIFT. It's possible for those who are willing to be intentional. I chose to change my watch, and you will have to decide to change your mindset as well. Whatever you do, accept the challenge and don't reject the feelings, energy, and potential of what life can offer. I want you to believe that you can make every day a Winsday! But know this, it will not just happen, so you must be intentional in your thinking to manifest these thoughts in your life.

WINNING YOUR BEST LIFE

Finish the following sentences:

1. My mindset that I must address is ...

2. My power phrase will be ...

3. The person that challenges me the most is ...

4. To move forward, I need to..

Are you operating from an old mindset? Take some time to think about the area of your life that you would like to see change. In this area, I challenge you to activate a power phrase and allow it to influence your conversations and choices. Monitor the changes that occur. Revisit this section when you feel you are not moving forward and remind yourself to update your thoughts just as you update your phone to the latest operating system.

Chapter 2

Challenging the L's

"Limits can be lifted, lowered, or left alone; you decide."

*W*hy do you keep stopping at the same point? It's the thought I had in my head and, thank God I didn't let it come out of my mouth. Now, for those who don't know me, you must understand I'm super competitive, and I want to win at everything. Let me set the context, and you'll understand why I couldn't say too much of anything.

It was a Thursday evening at Nova Gymnastics in Cedar Hill, Texas, when I realized that everyone has a limit they get to, and then, for some inexplicable reason, they stop. It was here where I would sit watching my daughter Sariyah practice gymnastics. She was only eight at the time, and she seemed to love every aspect of her first season of gymnastics, except her coach—now that's a story within a story. I'm not sure if what she loved best was jumping into the pit filled with Styrofoam cushions, or if it was climbing the rope that led to a bell tied to the roof's ceiling. All I knew was she never wanted to miss, and we had to be on time.

I used this time to wind down from another hectic day of sales. I tried to slow down, and, unlike me, I wouldn't answer my phone while I watched my daughter tumble, learn cartwheels, and attempt new things each week because I didn't want to miss anything. What I did know was every week Sariyah would climb and climb, and she would get to the same point—just as she always did—and stop, glance up and then down, and soon make her way back to the starting point. They were only allowed to attempt the rope once per session, and each week I knew this would be the week for a breakthrough. So, I began looking forward to the end of the session, and as any competitive father would do, I gave her the pep talk that would lead to her breakthrough. Unfortunately, when she reached that point of the rope, her motivation from the speech didn't move her beyond that same spot on the rope. What was it? Was she tired? Did she suddenly become afraid of heights? I could only imagine yet knowing my child, I knew I really couldn't dig deeper than the surface because I didn't want to come across as if I was disappointed. This was her rope to climb, and she was having fun climbing to that particular spot on the rope.

Could I really get that upset with her? It seemed so easy to coach, yet so difficult to live. I knew if she got that high on the rope, what would it be to pull up a few more inches, so she could finally ring that bell? I knew she was right there. I knew she could do it, but still, she didn't go past a certain point. It dawned on me that I understood her more than she even knows because I started examining my life, and I too had to ask myself: "What part of the rope do I stop at? Where's my limit? And, why do I not push beyond this comfortable place and give just a little more effort to break through, be, and become all I was intended to be?" You see, the conversation is easier to have when we are examining someone else's life. It's easier to sit back and see what others should do while we play it safe.

We all have choices when we face our lids. Are you tracking with me? **Our lids are our limits. Before we examine our choices, I want you to think about your rope and name your limit.** If you do this exercise, this chapter will lead to a breakthrough. Anytime I ask you to do something; I want you to see it action in me. One of my lids that I had to address was: I've waited too long to get started. Even though I'm in my early forties, I oftentimes battled with comparing my start to someone else's middle. Oh, how dangerous this can be. With the increase and advance of social media, keeping up with the latest filters can be a slippery slope that you and I should never travel down. You and I have one of three choices to make with our identified limit/lid. We can:

- leave them alone;

- unscrew and lift the lid;

- succeed by lowering our expectations.

What do you usually do? Which of the above choices do you find repeatedly choose? Sariyah seemed to be ok with leaving her lid alone. This became her safe zone. You've heard the saying, "How you do one thing is normally how you do all things?"

If you remember, I stated earlier in this chapter that Sariyah loved everything about gymnastics except for her coach. You may have wondered what was wrong with her coach? You see, Sariyah is my child, and we want to walk in number one and walk out number one. Sariyah's coach acknowledged what she did well, but he also saw where she could improve. He wasn't impressed with her gift only; he was committed to her development. Sariyah, I want you to know I understand what you were feeling because I had to learn this one right here. Coaches challenge the best version of myself. Coaches speak to the potential within. Coaches address the blind spots. Coaches are committed to making me better. Every once and awhile, there should be a sting after being challenged by your coach.

Here is an example in my own life. It's VIP Day at my first *Speak and Write* experience, when I get called out of the crowd and requested to join the G.O.A.T. of Communication Lisa Nichols on her stage. So, I don't' get in trouble by someone who may have thought I just took a stab at my coach, let me explain: G.O.A.T. stands for Greatest of All Time. If you haven't had the privilege of hearing Coach speak, please find some time to visit youtube and type in Lisa

Nichols. For some, I would have to tell you which message to listen to, but for Lisa, you can just take your pick. This is the stage I now find myself on, and this is the individual that says to me, "Speak on the subject of love. Go ahead and begin." Well, I'm not ever really nervous, so I open up my mouth and outflows some words in my rhythmic tone with a few rhyming words mixed in. As soon as I neared my conclusion, the audience gave me the noise I like: some handclaps and a few okay's. Immediately, Coach Lisa raised her left hand and quieted them down and said, "That would've been good for most, but for you, that's playing it safe."

Ugggggggh. Are you kidding me? You brought me out to San Diego, California, to do this? Now mind you, we're not on the white sandy beach enjoying the sizzling sun or enjoying the sounds of a live band while drinking a Mai Tai. No, we're locked in a hotel conference room from sunup to sundown learning about the science of communication, and Lisa's 17 techniques on how to be an effective communicator.

On numerous occasions, Coach had stated to me on that I've finally met my match when I met her. She said, "I understand your talent because I was you ten years ago. I'm not going to allow you to get away with giving the world your 70% and impressing people when I know there's greater locked up within you."

Don't we all need this type of confrontation and accountability to break beyond our current barriers or limits that hold us back from experiencing the life we so long for?

Before we move any further, please repeat this statement: I have the power to create the future I want, regardless of my past. Please understand that *regardless* means that there is nothing in my yesterday that I can't overcome in my today. I must commit to addressing it rather than avoiding it.

My good friend, Johnny Collins, says this, "Your *lack of* should not stop your *in spite of*." I've seen and met too many successful individuals who overcame a rough start. As a child, I was pulled out of class daily to work with a speech pathologist. Yes, the one you may have seen on TV, the one on Facebook Lives, me—working on talking. Isn't it funny how the very thing that could be our excuse gets turned into our instrument of breakthrough? I'll go more into my story later with the chapter entitled *Excuses or Excuse Me,* but you don't know how badly I want to stop right here and tell you that the Creator created you with unique abilities—one being the ability to bounce back. Right where you are, in the face of your pain, with tears rolling down your cheeks, or with both fists clenched, you need to know you were born to win. You can learn it, leave it, lose it, or use it to make your next move your best move.

Okay! I have to say this now, so no one reading can later say, "I am where I am because I wasn't given the opportunity to be anything else." I am a realist, an optimist and, most importantly, I am an opportunist. I believe we have all been given an opportunity to create the future. My future is created daily based on my conversations and my choices. Will you acknowledge the lids that have become your limits? They are different for each of us, but we all have some lid that has been placed over our lives. You will never go beyond the level that you choose to believe is possible for your life. I can't want it for you, see it in you, nor tell you it's possible, but until you loosen that limiting belief and replace it with a new belief system, you will remain capped.

Don't equate saying something as believing something. It begins with our words, but our words must be cemented and surrounded by faith and action. I've said plenty of things that sounded good that I wanted to believe. Maybe that's the camp of "fake it 'til you make it" folks. I believe in saying it until you believe it and behaving as you believe, and one day, you will see what you believe.

Let's talk about how we can raise our lids and develop a new belief system.

1. **I must first acknowledge the lids that are over my life; honest assessment is critical.** I'm not talking about social media honest. I'm talking about pulling the covers back honest. I call this clarity. Clarity is when we take a 360-degree view of what is. I purposely want to describe this because those who may struggle as I did with clarity miss this step in the process. I told myself negative things about myself for so long; I started to believe what I was saying, even though they weren't true. I know it's sad, but it's just the truth. Our minds will believe what we speak as truth, regardless of

whether it's true or not. At this moment, I learned a valuable lesson, and that is exactly step number two.

2. **Reframe your world with a new power statement.** What is it that you want to see or be? Here is where we must become specific. As a kid, I told you I struggled with accepting the Creator's creation. I didn't love my skin color; I hated that I stuttered, and I didn't like what I saw in the mirror—a gap as wide as the Red Sea. These things shaped and formed an acceptance issue that I dealt with by overachieving and always trying to excel, so no one, including myself, would focus on any of my limiting beliefs. When someone said, "You're handsome," I didn't believe them. My limiting belief became if they knew about all of me, they wouldn't truly accept me.

My negative self-image was disguised by a shell of success. I stayed on the surface with individuals, and from an early age, I had a gift of controlling the conversation. I rarely let anyone inside of my inner space. I knew that if they got too close, they would see the not-so-pretty side of me, and I didn't know how to deal with this place. Let me explain.

Being a military child, we traveled often, so I blamed my lack of friends on our three-year travel schedule. All of my formative years, until the 7th grade, we traveled every three years. So, this should've ended when we moved to Arlington, Texas, and I grew up going to the same school with the same kids for the next five years of my life. Did it end? Of course, not. This had become a limiting belief. Now in the meantime, I won MVP of my basketball team, Mr. Boles Jr. High, Homecoming King, All-State in basketball, scholarship offers to over 28 schools and many more accolades of success. But quietly in this secret space, I couldn't stand the skin I was in. Now, how do you tell that to people who would die to have what I had? All I ever heard was, "Derrick, you're so gifted, and you're gonna do so many great things." And I would lay on my bed and think *if they only knew the real you and your real thoughts.*

This thought followed me throughout my work career, and, as you know, **we learn to live with our limp**. We find our coping mechanisms and stay around the "safe" place. For me, it was success and controlling conversations, as well as the lack of depth in friendships. The easiest way to stay on the surface is always to be moving and meeting new people. I never kept a friendship nor a relationship. (I'll tell that story later.) I sucked in this area of my life. You have to remember; I needed too much validation and affirmation for me to ever understand how to give to someone else what they may need from me. On the outside, it seemed like I did have what they needed because people would always come to me for answers. I was known as "the guru," or even to some as "Baby Jesus." Sounds cute, but looking back on it, I understand the reasons why now. It wasn't until I realized people don't care how much you know until they know how much you care. I had to genuinely care beyond the content about the people I connected to.

This may be the reason I walked out on my first marriage. I failed. In the beginning, before any of my issues surfaced, I was fine, but once I had to deal with me or at least see me, I didn't know what to do. It's easier to run to the next and begin from the beginning, rather than deal with the underdeveloped areas of our lives. It's easier to show off your good and keep people shielded from your authentic self. As I mature, I look back at my youthful self and just shake my head. Presenting perfect is a recipe for ultimate disaster. I think it's why I spend more of my time talking about my mistakes. I never want to have this type of ending for anyone again, at least if I can control it. I've owned up to my mistakes. I've asked forgiveness and have moved on. Moving on doesn't mean there weren't repercussions for my decisions. Most know that the rock thrown in the river will disrupt the water, but what you don't know is how many ripple effects will vibrate from the occurrence.

Maybe I understand this a little better than some because of my time in sales. You see, there's a difference between cost and value. The cost is what you paid for an item, but the value is what you deem it's worth to be. Different things are more valuable to some than others. You get to determine the value of your peace. Your breakthrough. Your next level living. The next version of your life. Slow down, please, and think about some areas that you say are important in your life. Ask yourself a few questions: How much does this area of my life cost me? And if you're bold enough, ask the question what is it worth to me? It's these types of questions that help us make destiny decisions.

Let me not run too fast without providing additional insight into where I was mentally while going through this dark time in my life. Divorce may have been decided, but honestly, it wasn't desired. Who really desires divorce? So how did I get here? Easy answer and that is when you take your eye off the ball, it rarely hits the bat. It was this statement that I heard that I should've known to drop that got me into a whole lot of trouble.

Now, at the time of the statement, I laughed, thinking to myself, "That's funny." And then, later, I realized my hard heart had somewhere adopted the statement, and it led me to places I never thought I'd go and eventually to making decisions I didn't see myself making. You're probably wondering what is this statement? What does it have to do with challenging our limits? Well, first let me give you the statement, then I'll share how it's relevant to leaders today. The statement was, "I got my sin under control." That's it. Simply put, I can manage through my mess. Okay, don't leave me out here by myself. Have you ever felt like you could handle your hang-up? I'm speaking about the issue you keep justifying by saying to yourself, "I only do it…Everyone has something they struggle with…" I get it, we all do have some area of our lives that we need to better manage. Just because it's sensitive and fragile doesn't mean it can't be addressed and challenged. Maybe, it's my time, my finances, my career, my hobbies, or a mixture of all the above. The is a precaution to everyone reading not to allow any area of our lives to go unattended. What we sweep that we should've killed will grow up and become the monster that brings us nightmares.

I thought I could control my situation to the point I was juggling two sides, two stories, and two expectations. Do you know how hard it is to attempt to please two opposite and opposing forces? If you've ever tried, you know what I'm referring to here, and for those of you who haven't, please don't attempt this way of living.

The moment humility leaves, arrogance appears. The humble individual is grateful for where they are and open to growing into who they need to be, while the arrogant focuses on the outer giftings and forget their shit stinks, too. Did I go there? I'm sorry if I offended you, but I wanted to get your attention for a brief minute. Sometimes, you just have to hear it the way that it is. I fell victim to my inability and unwillingness to acknowledge clarity within. Let me remind you of our definition of clarity? Clarity is when I take a 360-degree view of what is, and wisdom picks one thing to focus on to improve the quality of one's life. You see, my character didn't just change because I kept living. I had to acknowledge the cracks in my character and intentionally begin addressing the concerns with honesty and integrity. It will only change when you decide to change.

The power of this principle is you can use this to change you, and you can also use this same principle to change your business. Now that I've done the work in me, it makes it a bit easier to spot it in others. I'm really good at dealing with talented people because I received my Master's in building back my shattered character. If

I could do it with all of my issues, I'm sure we'll be okay assisting you.

I speak as a person who received grace. Isn't it sad when the very individuals that needed grace when they were rebuilding forget to offer it when others are rebuilding? At Assist U2 Win, the environment for vulnerability is celebrated and protected. Game Changers need a place where they don't have to have it all together; they don't have to give all the right responses; they can be authentic and receive the space to heal. This environment also challenges the individual to confront it, change it, and carry on knowing that one day, you'll use it as your superpower to assist others to win.

I love what my coach Lisa Nichols says, "Don't sit in your story and wallow, stand on your story and win." Okay, I added the win part. That's what she meant to say, or that's what I heard her say. Are you ready to unlock your destiny by addressing any specific areas in your life? The paycheck for working on this project is a life free from guilt and shame of an experience that can no longer define or confine your life.

WINNING YOUR BEST LIFE

Finish the following sentences:

1. The area I need to confront is…

2. Today, I'm deciding not to stop in the following area…

3. Taking one more step looks like…

Be willing to confront and challenge your limits. **Why do you stop where you stop?** I want you to challenge yourself to trust yourself. If you can get to this point, can't you get to the next point? Even if you're at the highest point in your circle, challenge yourself to go one more step. One more will lead to another level. I promise you'll enjoy the view when you get there.

Chapter 3

When Out Is Better Than Safe

"I must become comfortable with being uncomfortable."

Baseball was my thing. From the age of four 'til 13 years old, I seemed to always be around the game of baseball. I love every aspect of the game—from the hot, sticky days in the park to the dollar dogs at Dodger Stadium, and you can't forget the scenery of the palm trees in the outfield. As you can see, this game of baseball shaped my life and my winning mindset. I hit leadoff, which meant I hit first in the lineup. I always got things started. Maybe that's why I am the loudest, boldest, and bravest person in the room—at least, most of the time. But it wasn't always like this.

There was a time, most don't know about when I couldn't stand looking in the mirror while brushing my teeth. I had a gap y'all—and not just some attractive, manly, Michael Strahan-sized gap, but I'm talking about separating the Red Sea type of gap. As a kid, I only remember the name-calling—

the noise—that surrounded my gap. It lasted long enough, and often enough, that I had to get used to it, or the noise would've caused me to retaliate by doing something that I know I would later regret.

I both hated and loved that noise. There was the noise of celebration, and then there was the internal noise of aggravation. Some cheered for me, while others laughed at me. Because I was able to smile at the noise, no one really knew that I had grown both addicted to and numb to the noise that surrounded my life.

Let me pause and stay here for just a second. **What noise do you want to hear desperately? And what noise are you trying to drown out? What noise motivates you to perform? And what noise has paralyzed your progress? What noise makes you feel bigger than life? And what noise has invaded your space and left you feeling less than, not worthy of, and like it will never happen? Have you identified your noise?** I know I'm unique, but I know I'm not alone when I refer to this noise. You know the noise. It comes as a scream from certain individuals and as a whisper when you can't sleep. The noise that finds a way of speaking even in silence. The noise is one that FloJo can't outrun, nor can Tiger Woods drive away. It's the noise that walks with you, and the noise that talks to you. I never thought I would sign up for reoccurring payments of this noise as if it's an episode on my Netflix account. How could I push pause? How could I silence the noise that seemed to steal my inner peace and sabotage my feelings of significance? Have you ever had success and suffering mixed together? This is that feeling that's hard to explain. On the one hand, things are looking up, but on the other, you're miserable. While people are celebrating you, you smile, wanting it to both continue and end. This inner turmoil not dealt with properly is what drives our suicide rates higher and higher.

Baseball brought me a different noise, a noise of cheers when I made a play at shortstop, and a noise of thunderous celebration as I rounded third base, moving my little legs quickly to score once again. Baseball gave me a noise that I loved, needed, and got addicted to. This noise came to compete against the noise of dealing with the dark side of Derrick. All I ever did was live my life for the noise of success. I learned to give people what they wanted, and in return, I expected and waited for the noise of approval. My acceptance was somewhere wrapped inside of their noise. The louder it was, the greater I felt.

I've never been strung out on drugs, but I know the feeling because I was strung out on noise. Who else relates to my issue? Maybe yours isn't noise, but can you identify what you desire to experience in order to feel whole and complete? Is it a relationship? A house? A car? Designer clothes? A certain title on your job? Whatever it is, you know that you need it. Maybe that's why some people crop, cut, and paste what they want others to see on social media. Maybe they, or we, do it because we all want to show a certain thing because we need people to give us our noise. I need one more like, one more share (and when we're honest, we're looking for a certain person to like and share it), but just one more may be enough to put our phone down until the next time the high is needed.

I'm sorry; I know we're talking about how to design the life you love, not how to deal with your issues. I know, **but how do you design the life you love without dealing with the noise that clouds it?**

Now, we have to get back to Little League. I learned many lessons from my sporting days, and I appreciate the players and the coaches I met along the journey. However, I must say this lesson has been the most eye-opening lesson that Little League teaches many, and they may not know how this is impacting lives still today. I saw it in me, and I see it in my son, Torin.

Torin is the middle child who loves baseball, as well. Guess what? He and I both hit leadoff. Torin is extremely fast, and, with that being said, he can hit balls in the infield, and most of the time, he's called safe at first base.

Well, on this occasion, we were in a tournament in San Antonio, Texas, and Torin was up to bat. He hit a dribbler down the third baseline, and he ran down the line while the third baseman was charging the ball. The third baseman bare-handed the ball and slung it over to the first baseman. Mind you; the boy made a big-league play. At the same time, the ball hit the mit, Torin's left foot touched the outer portion of the bag. We call this a "bang-bang" type of play. Seriously, we needed a slow cam and instant replay to get this call right, but in an instant, we expected the umpire to make a call. He was either going to be safe or out. There was no in-between.

The umpire's noise that comes from his mouth was getting ready to determine our mood and feelings. If we're called safe, then it's an instant celebration, but if he calls him out, it's going to be immediate frustration. There's no in-between when dealing with this noise. Just as the umpire must make a call, so too must you decide which way it's going to be. I wish we could, but we know we can't tell life to give me a second; I'll get back to you. Just like the umpire is expected to decide in an instant, so must you and me.

The umpire said, "He's out." I wish Tyler Perry Studios was present. I would've been the producer and leading actor because both Torin and I put on a show. I was the first base coach on his select baseball team, 817 Sports. I jumped in the air like **no way**, while Torin threw both hands up in the air in utter disgust and sheer disappointment all because he felt he was safe, even though he was called out.

Noise speaks, "Man, we don't get breaks in life." Noise says, "Life will always call you out." Your parents divorced; you didn't finish college; there's not enough money in your savings; you had a baby in your teenage years, and, on and on, the noise speaks. With all this noise being played, the whisper of Little League shared a principle that most miss. We focus on what the noise is saying, while I've learned to hear what is not being said. If I ask Torin or, better yet, any baseball player this one question, I will get 90% of them to give me the same response. Question: Were you safe or out? They are always going to tell me; I was safe. And, there it is. Little League taught in a subtle, simple way that safe is better than out.

Who wants to be out?

Out of the circle of friends?

Out of your comfort zone?

Out in front?

Out of working capital? No one does.

We all want to be safe. Maybe it wasn't Little League, but can you relate to the lesson of wanting to play it safe. You make safe calls, safe decisions, safe risks, and safe statements. You have learned to play it safe. Safe is small. Safe is routine. Safe is controlled. Safe is your norm.

I am going to challenge you to stop playing safe and start going all out. We are getting out of our comfort zones, and we will live life in the challenge zone. We are getting out from behind our baggage and noise, and we are renaming and reshaping our world with new words, new beliefs, and new actions. We will get out of our own way and stop hiding from the success that's been looking for us.

When we get out of our own way, we will finally experience a new level of winning.

WINNING YOUR BEST LIFE

Finish the following sentences:

1. I have not played full out because...

2. My biggest fear is that if I play full out...

3. I want to begin playing full out in the following areas...

4. Because I've decided to play full out ...

Safe is safe. Do it afraid. Go big or stay home. Begin. Start. Continue. Now Finish. You owe it to yourself and to your Creator to give us the full expression of who you are. Anything less would be selfish and not the best use of your existence.

Chapter 4

The Courage of Las Vegas

"Insanity and destiny do not go together."

It's known as "Sin City." To me, it's the place where I watch the Super Bowl every year. One of the fascinating things about being in Las Vegas during Super Bowl weekend is the gathering of the gamblers. You know, the individuals who are willing to risk it to receive it. As much as you don't think you're one, you are gambling every day of your own life. It may not feel the same because you're not pulling down some penny slot, nor tapping your finger asking for another card on the blackjack table, but the ability to create our future is found in our choices and conversations. This is where we become a gambler every day.

Whom you choose to or not to talk to is a gamble. The application you fill out and the position you desire are a gamble. Do I leave where I am to enter a new company? Will the promises of additional pay outweigh the traffic to drive to the other side of town? It's these choices and conversations that cause many to live a life of comfort with the feeling of boredom that tempts us to do something different ever so often.

I love Las Vegas, and I plan a few trips a year to the city that never sleeps. I always leave with a valuable lesson. Let's start with the 2018 comeback of the century: Atlanta Falcons up at half-time by over 21 points, and the game is over—at least we thought.

At half-time, I walked over to the line where you place your bets on the second half. I can recall the conversation I had with two men whose names I never received. "You got to bet big on New England Patriots in the second half." I said, "What?" *Were these guys crazy? Had they been watching the game I was watching?* I wondered.

To quickly remind my non-football fans, Atlanta dominated every aspect of this football game up to that point. It looked like the game was over, but it was only half-time. I must stop and encourage someone whom has dominated thus far by life.

I realize if we were talking one to another, you could tell the story in such a way that I'd be convinced the next thing that happened in your story would be another letdown. I understand the string of luck you've received thus far, and I can even empathize with you on why you're feeling down and discouraged. (I wanted to say but, right then. So, let me say it now) **But**, I have to tell you, life isn't over yet. Remember, I left you in chapter two with my life down in the dumps because of the decisions I had made.

The first step in a comeback is taking responsibility for where you are without giving excuses. The excuse will cause you to blame others when the actual person to blame is your inability to make quality choices. Hard pill to swallow, but you must take the medicine if you want to have a "bounce back" experience.

The New England Patriots went into the locker room down on the scoreboard, but up in their minds. I'm not sure what the speech was, but I do know it resulted in a team deciding to finish the game and find a way out of what they had allowed to happen. There's that message of motivation inside of us all. Unfortunately, it's not yelling like a cheerleader, yet, it's whispering like the wind on a chilly night. It speaks to those who will listen, and when you decide to use your struggle as your strength, you will realize your predicament is just a set up for your great comeback. While I was down, I knew I wasn't made for this. I knew there were better days in front of me, not just behind me. I knew I could climb and rise above the mess that I created. I knew it, but where would I begin?

The two men said to bet on New England. I learned at that moment if you're going to bet, make sure you bet on the right team. Don't miss this moment. This is the time for you to understand that you are the right team. You are worthy of someone putting their chips on the line because they believe your setback is showcasing your comeback. Let me be crystal clear when I say, "Bet on you."

I have been known for the following statement: **You build what you birth, and you drop what you adopt.** Too many times in our lives, we bet on others. We bet on our jobs versus our dreams, our bosses versus our thoughts, and we settle for living someone else's dream, instead of allowing our employer to be our best investor. I'm not telling you that everyone is supposed to be an entrepreneur, but I am telling you that you shouldn't remain where you're tolerated when someone wants to celebrate you and your giftedness. Will you decide today that you are worth betting on?

So, what does that look like? Maybe, you can begin by scheduling a get-a-way. This is when you take off and don't tell anyone where you're going, so you can do you. Get a massage; check into a hotel; take a bubble bath; play a round of golf; smoke a cigar; go shopping; take yourself out for a drink; watch a movie, or binge-watch something on Netflix, etc. I think you get the point. Until you make yourself a priority, you won't be a priority.

Life has a way of always giving you more to do than you have time to do it in. I believe it was at a John Maxwell seminar when John shared the principle of the 3 Rs. He told us to ask ourselves three questions, and the answers to these questions would help us streamline what we are doing, so we could get more done doing less. Here are the questions:

1. What is required of you and you only?

2. What gives you the greatest return?

3. What brings you the greatest reward?

If you will take the time to answer these questions, you will find that we are busy doing things we can delegate. Some things on our calendar can be immediately eliminated, leaving us with only a few things we should be doing. From this, I've begun coming up with my daily MVP – Most Valuable Priority. I must share something about the word priority.

The word "priority" derives from a Latin word, and from the inception of the word, it had a singular focus. It wasn't until the mid-1900's when we made this word plural. Now, you have people walking around with priorities when the original use of the word was simply priority. I've adopted the original intention, along with Gary Keller's book: *The One Thing*. The combination of these two principles has helped me streamline my daily activities for higher productivity.

In the car business, I worked many hours, and the expectation was always to work just one more. It didn't matter if you'd just finished a 12-hour day; they had the expectation for you to work just one more hour. As I came to the end of my career, I became vocal about my time and my schedule. I remember meeting with my Market President, and he asked, "Did you leave already?" I answered directly and said, "Yes, sir." He gave me a quick one-liner and out of my mouth, without any thought, I said, "I'm not trying to win the trophy for the most hours worked."

I pride myself on showing my clients how to do less yet achieve more. It's in the ability to obtain clarity that one can achieve effectiveness. The Pareto Principle states, 20% of our effort produces 80% of our return. Once we identify the right 20%, we must maximize our knowledge and skill, and we will see Ten times the results and the increase.

Let me tell you one more story of Las Vegas before shifting gears. I have many, but I don't want to bore you with my adventures. This event happened in 2019, so it's probably pretty recent in relation to when this book is released. My wife and my cousin, Manuel, decided to go out on the strip, walking around. I stayed behind playing Blackjack. Oh, how I love the game of Blackjack. It's so thrilling when I can double down and get the right card or the dealer busts, and I can say 24 – Marshawn Lynch. (I have a saying for every dealer bust card.)

While my wife was on the strip, she sent me a text saying she was about to get a tattoo. Now, you must know she says this every year, and every year we come home, and she doesn't have any additional tattoos. So, I replied, "Sounds good." Well, this year was different. Somehow, while they were roaming the streets, they ran into Mr. Tattoo. This guy had tattoos everywhere: his forehead, fingers, arms, etc. To my surprise, my wife ended up getting a tattoo, and I was amazed that I liked it.

Now, up until this time, I've always been against tattoos. Not because of my religious upbringing, but more because I couldn't see paying for pain. Well, at dinner, I kept looking at the tattoo, and I kept asking questions about the experience. She picked up on it and said, "You ought to get you one." I quickly shut that thought down with an emphatic, "*No*," even though in my mind, I thought this would be cool. So, throughout dinner, I kept talking with myself, debating what I would get if I did get one.

The next morning was our last day in Las Vegas. We went and ate at this chicken and waffle spot, and then walked the strip. Time was ticking, and my mind was racing. Up until this point, I had lived my life safe. I was always worried about how someone would perceive me and if my actions would hinder the desires of my heart. You must remember, I had already jacked up my life through my choices, and I didn't want to go through all of that again. I had to learn how to succeed safely. Someone's saying, "There's nothing wrong with that." And you're absolutely right, but for me, I just didn't want that to be my life. Remember, I'm the gambler. I wanted to get back to living my life, betting on me, and be willing to risk it all for what I believed. So, at that moment, I said, "I wonder what a tattoo would look like on me."

As I was making that statement, I noticed a girl with a sign asking who wanted a temporary tattoo inside of Planet Hollywood. I looked at her and thought *this is the perfect thing for a guy like me. I can see what it looks like, and if I like it, I can plan to get one in the future; if I don't, then it will go away.* So, I stopped and said, I want one. Now, the grown man in me still wanted to know would this experience hurt, and both she and my wife got a kick out of making me feel bad for asking.

So, what would I put on my body? This question had to be answered with something that means everything to you without any doubt nor regret. Tattoos are meant to be a symbol of something that holds great significance to you. Now, I'd had almost a day to think about it, and I knew exactly what I would put on my body. If I was going to do this, I wanted my why, my reason for existence, my gamble—my everything—to be a symbol, a sign, and a statement of what I stand for.

With that in mind, I scrolled to a photo on my phone of Assist U2 Win. She, within minutes, had this mark of Assist U2 Win on my right arm, and I absolutely loved it. It was chilly, and I had on long sleeves, but to make myself feel like a "real gangsta'" I had one sleeve rolled up, so everyone passing by could see my new tattoo of Assist U2 Win. You know, I had one problem, though. This tattoo was temporary. I liked it, and in days it was going to come off. I didn't want this, nor did I want this for my life. I was tired of feeling something and doing it while I felt it, knowing the feeling was going to wear off. I was tired of changing like Texas weather. I needed something of permanence. I knew Assist U2 Win was greater than just a feeling; it was and is my reason for living. I wake thinking about who I can assist to win. I go to bed thinking about who I helped, and how can I grow this brand. I told you before I hate losing, and I know people hate the feeling of being a loser. That's why I strive daily to motivate and inspire action that results in winning.

"Tamara, call your tattoo guy and see if he can get me in before we leave," I said. The courage to do it came over me, and I knew it was now or never. Too many times, when we have the courage to act, we allow the forces that oppose us to slow us down, make us question, or even second guess what we know. I learned **in my life that massive, immediate, imperfect action is better than a well thought out**

plan that has no action. Tamara called, and my man said he'd get us in if we came over right away.

We caught an Uber to his office, and an hour later—on my left arm—I had a permanent tattoo, while my right arm had the temporary one. As we end this chapter, I have to ask you this pondering question: Have you declared and decided to walk toward your dream with a no matter what mentality? Lisa Nichols, my coach, says, "No matter what." It's the only way to build what you birth. It's the only way to step out of your yesterday and into your future. It's the only way to leave what's good in order to move towards what's great. And lastly, it's the only way to leave great when greater is calling your name. How can you begin putting this into action? Courage. The courage of Las Vegas.

It takes courage to step out of your comfort zone and to do something you've never done before. It takes courage to bet on you. It takes courage to risk it all on your dreams. It takes courage to take a step. Las Vegas may be Sin City for others, but to me, it stands for the place of courage. I see people wearing things you can only get away with in Vegas; people drink more than they should, and it's the place where I went from temporary to permanent with my vision of building Assist U2 Win.

WINNING YOUR BEST LIFE

Finish the following sentences:

1. My plan of action in this area of my life is …

2. I will take care of myself the following day…

Let's think about things you wanted to do that you haven't done yet. Will you pick one thing this week and put a plan of action to it? You're the author of your life, so make sure it's something you want to do. This could be treating yourself to a spa day, taking a trip alone, or forgiving a friend. Take courage from this chapter and begin to implement it immediately.

PART TWO:

METHODS FOR

MOVEMENT

Productivity is experienced when I commit priority to the right activity.

Chapter 5

What is Leadership?

"Every person is born. Every leader is developed."

Leadership is influence—nothing more and nothing less. Most times, when the question, "What is leadership?" comes up, a series of answers roll out of people's mouths. Using many words, most people describe the characteristics of leadership, tell who was influential in their lifetime, or even speak about their desire to be a great leader. When broken down to one thing, leadership is centered on having the ability to influence another person or group. This can be done at home, at church, on your job, in a beauty salon, or on a sports team. When it's all said and done, it takes one person influencing another.

I was a loudmouth growing up. Ask my wife today, and she'll tell you that I do run out of words. When you talk for a living, it's hard to believe that I can run out of words. By the end of the day, I just don't want to talk, so I've learned to lead without talking. When I deal with our dog Smokie, I don't use words like most people do. I use my fingers to snap. When I snap, he responds. The running joke in our home is the person who likes him the least has the most influence and control. I said this to show one principle: *the loudmouth may always be heard, but that doesn't mean they are always listened to and followed.*

Influence is earned over time. We all have the seed of influence; yet, we all don't invest it in the same way. This is probably the best time to point out that leadership can be both positive and negative. Remember, we are talking about influence. Reading through history, we've seen good leaders, and we've all witnessed some examples of poor leadership. Before we judge too quickly the people who followed bad examples of leadership, remember, once one has gained influence, they can steer an individual based on their heart's motivation.

Everyone who leads must answer the questions of who, why, and how they are going to lead. I've always stated that leadership gives you a platform to showcase what's in your heart right now. If you're a giver, you give. If you're a helper, you help. If you're a leader, you lead. You should already be doing what you say you want to do before anyone deems you as such.

Like many other skills, one can develop into a better version. We must devote our energy, time, and resources to our development. While some individuals possess natural giftings, no one was born a leader, we were all born as babies. I've committed to daily growing in some areas of leadership, which allows me to increase my influence.

When it comes to leading people, you must remember you can be on different levels of leadership with different people. Don't make the cardinal mistake of thinking there's a One Size Fits All shirt when it comes to leadership. You must identify what level you're on and make it a point to move levels as soon as possible.

Let's begin with the first level of leadership, and that is Title Only Leaders. A "Title Only" leader is the lowest form of leadership. Following because "I have to" versus because "I want to" is no greater than you telling me that I must marry that person your parents just loved so much. You get the point. Leadership exercised out of titles are restricted to job descriptions and minimum standards. When you see people clocking in and clocking out without the thought of the big picture, just know they see you, and their position as a requirement, not a choice. The good news is knowing this tells you what you must do in order to move them to action and move out of this level of leadership.

In order to begin making your first move up the leadership ladder, I want you to think about adding value to the individual you desire to lead. This seems like it's so obvious, but it's difficult to do because the return is not seen immediately. If you examine the number one reason why people leave their jobs, it isn't the paycheck being too small; it's the lack of connection and value that they feel from their employers. People don't leave organizations; they leave individuals. Do you want to last a lifetime? I know you do, and so do I, so make it a point to focus on adding value to others. When I want to add value to your life, I must think more about you and your needs rather than my agenda. This type of connection allows an individual to begin the process of true buy-in.

Charismatic individuals think this is our strength, but I would easily share what you think is buy-in is simply just a head nod of confession. Confession can be defined as an agreement. When employees head nod, they many times are acknowledging hearing what you're saying, and it's misinterpreted as buy in. Maybe five years ago, I listened to a presentation, and the presenter dropped this nugget that I've never forgotten, "Until there's weigh-in, there's not true buy-in." I didn't take the time to create the space for my people to share their thoughts, and we sure didn't have time to go back in forth over our feelings. So, I thought. When I began taking the time with my people to actively listen to what's important to them on day one, then I moved levels of leadership with the right heart.

Today, I have a team of leaders around me who not only give me their hands; they also have given me their hearts. The word that may come to mind is loyalty. I may not be all the way there quite yet, but the foundation is being poured out through consistent actions. Recently, I've taught this principle of adding value to my coaching clients. Here are a few nuggets from this lesson: When our value exceeds the expectations of people, you'll always get the opportunity. This is one of my favorite quotes when it comes to value. Let me give you one more before we move on, "Value is being determined by everything you do."

What you say is important. How you say it is remembered. Teach me something new, and I'll probably need a refresher course soon. Make me feel valuable, and I'll remember you for a lifetime. With that, great leaders find ways to always add value to those they encounter.

Mother Teresa is a great example of leadership in action. This familiar phrase is coined because of her, ***"People don't care how much you know until they first know how much you care."*** The people she served, daily, knew her motives for serving were about their benefit and not hers. From raising money to needing volunteers, Mother Teresa always had more than enough. When you make it about people, people will find a way to make it about you. This is totally opposite to the way our society thinks today. Most people lead from the W.I.I.F.M. approach. If you haven't heard that acronym, it means, "What's in It for Me?" We think what can I gain? Who will see me? How much more money will I make if I get them to say yes?

Making it about people goes against what society teaches today. Society currently reinforces selfishness that must be eradicated from one's heart if you're going to lead with integrity and longevity. We've all been around individuals about whom we kept saying, "Something's not right." We may not have been able to put our finger on it, but we just didn't feel they genuinely cared about our best interests.

Think about an employer that is a taskmaster. You just don't go the extra mile for this type of leader. You're there because of bills to pay, not because of the person or your passion. If the leader doesn't move beyond this level, people will soon begin to bail out on the company. Remember, people don't leave companies; people leave people. But, what about the leader who knows how to be relational before functional? This is the leader you grant permission to lead you. You want them to share things with you; you welcome it and look forward to their insight. This doesn't take place with a title only leader. This begins taking place with the next level of leader, which is a relational leader.

At this stage of leadership, the relational leader is giving more than his/her hands. They're giving and receiving from both their hands and their heart. This is seen in their actions. "I'll stay late today," or, "I don't mind coming in on my day off." These are statements you don't say to some egotistical, self - serving leader who has an agenda that includes using you like a pawn on a chessboard. People in this type of work environment only give until they find another place to work, to serve, or to operate in their purpose. So, ensure that in this stage of leadership your motives are pure. I say this because we are going to eventually begin talking about the work that is necessary in order to grow our influence. Remember, every time you see influence, you are witnessing leadership.

WINNING YOUR BEST LIFE

Finish the following sentences:

1.The three traits I admire are …

2.My daily plan of growth consists of …

3. I will do the following with the people I lead …

Are you taking your leadership seriously? Think about a leader you admire and respect. What are you doing to become better at the traits that inspire you? Leadership is a commitment to a daily growth plan. If you don't continue to do what is necessary to grow, you will find yourself losing your level of influence with those who are following you. Be intentional to ensure you are influential.

Chapter 6

LEADERSHIP ASSESSMENT

"Leaders are challenged directly when they receive the gift of assessments."

What's your birthday? Would you believe me if I told you that my birthday is before Jesus? Yes, it is. Since, I asked you I guess I better tell you that my birthday is December 24th. Leaders are not born; they are developed. Depending on who you are and how you lead, different characteristics are magnified in the life of a leader.

I've identified 12 common characteristics that great leaders possess. As you read through the list, I want you to grade yourself in each of the categories. For the bold leader, have a dialogue with someone, and allow them to grade you in each of the categories we are going to discuss. Two points of caution:

1. Be open and receptive to their feedback.
2. No retaliation. Don't give them the "stank eye," or silent treatment, for answering the questions honestly. Feedback is an

opportunity to see life from another's perspective and it allows you to adjust as needed.

Don't forget we are human beings not human doings. There's a difference in being and doing. Let me tell you; I wish we were in a room doing this as a group exercise because I've witnessed many breakthroughs occur as we discuss each point of emphasis. For those who decide to take our Winsday 365 Coaching Course, I will provide detailed feedback in each area below. In the meantime, grade yourself using a scale of 0-5, 0 being the not too good, and 5 being self-mastery.

- Active listening skills;
- Aware of the "what" and "why" of one's life;
- An attitude that is infectious;
- Art of connecting and communicating;
- Appreciate the process (i.e. the problems and the promise);
- Attentive to the needs of others;
- You apply what others deny;
- You accept and allow failure;

- You appreciate your associations;

- You attract whatever you need to succeed.

Each of these ingredients can be developed with the implementation of proven principles. Let me tell you it takes work to be an effective leader. This is more than a title and a box of business cards. We are talking about steering the ship, not standing on the deck.

I tell people often that leading and managing are just not the same. For years, we used this term synonymously. They are similar, but they are not the same. How you define determines what you assign. Managing is, at best, keeping things afloat. Where leading is moving the needle. Both are vital and necessary in business. For now, we are discussing leadership, which in my opinion is the greater of the two.

As you read through the list, you'll probably grind your teeth in a few areas. How can I become all of these traits, so I can move up the ladder of leadership? Just *wanting* to move up is admirable. So, here's been my proven system for implementing new principles in my life.

1. Pick one area to focus on at a time. Picking too many areas can make this daunting task feel overwhelming. Getting better every day must become the expectation versus being all these things tomorrow.

2. Commit one solid month of effort. It sounds like this process is going to take forever, but I can assure you that learning less and applying more will get you further than trying to become an overnight success. If you adopt this approach, you will learn 12 new principles a year that will be understood and seen in your life.

3. Utilize the S.M.A.R.T. goal lab. This is an effective technique to ensure growth in the area of your choice. ***If it's not measurable; it won't be deliverable.***

4. Record your progress. I'm a firm believer in tracking your success. Don't forget to praise progress as a success. Excellence is the continual pursuit of getting better.

5. Repeat the process, month after month, until you experience mastery in each of these vital characteristics. Repetition is the foundation for mastery.

WHAT IS REQUIRED OF YOU AND ONLY YOU?

This is the grounding question that I come back to when I sense my life getting out of balance. We all, from time-to-time, take on too many projects. If it's not too many projects, maybe it's the wrong projects. In either case, I didn't function from a place of responsibility around this question; instead, I functioned out of impulse, the need for approval, or the desire to be viewed as a superhero.

When I say yes to projects I know I should say no to, I must dig deeper to learn why I'm saying yes and not just give a quick answer of, "I'll say no next time." When I begin to dig, I realized there are certain people, certain times, and certain projects I tend to fall for every time. When I asked myself the tough questions, here is what I found out about myself.

I have moved too quickly, and my heart is too big. This is not a bad thing, but from a workload perspective, it causes me to overcommit to people and projects that I should've had no business doing from the start. I realized it's mainly the Hero Syndrome that gets me into the most trouble. I think I can, when I should know I can't. I want everyone to see my greatness when sometimes they need to see my humanness.

I love this question because it teaches me how to work in my "sweet spot." The Pareto Principle states that a few tasks influence many of my results. To quantify this better, you may hear that 20% of our efforts produce 80% of our results. Think about this statement and really analyze it over your life. When I really began to believe and understand the Pareto Principle, I started adjusting my life to do less and still accomplish more. Did you get what I just dropped? There is a place where you can arrive that you'll be able to go from minus to multiply.

So, what will you do with the remaining tasks once you identify the ones you need to be doing? This is a great question, but we can't move to the remaining until we really understand how to identify the tasks we should keep. I promise to tell you what I do with my remaining tasks once we tackle finding your few tasks.

First of all, I have to credit the book *The One Thing* by Gary Keller and Jay Papasan as my guide to effectiveness. When I read this book, it adjusted my mindset, and I personally read this book twice per year. Without giving the movie ending away, the premise of this book asks, "What's the one thing I

This question takes the Pareto Principle and puts it on steroids. Instead of focusing on a few things, let's just focus on one thing. We are narrowing, so we can focus. With focus comes confidence. I am now going to be working in the place of my competence over my weakness. Why spend my best energy working on what I can't do? Instead, I spend it becoming an authority and an expert in my giftedness, and I'll soon tell you what to do with those weaknesses.

Now, let's magnify our brilliance and work diligently in this vein as much as possible. Remember, the question we started with asked, "What is required of you and only you?" To answer this question, you can take a sheet of paper out and just start listing the things that come to your head. This is exactly what we do when we are writing out our To-Do List; just first get them on paper.

Since we now we have them on paper, we are going to take our responsibility question and ask ourselves: Is this required of me and me only? Can anyone else do this? Matter-of-fact, do I need to be doing this? What results do I receive because of this task? These are just a few questions you can ask yourself to quickly identify if the task is needed or not. As I'm going through this process, here are the three things I'm going to choose between, and I'm going to write a one, two, or three next to each item.

1. Do it.
2. Delegate it.
3. Delete it.

All the items you write a one next to are now going to be regrouped. From this list, we are going to prioritize the list in order of importance until we identify our one thing. There is always one thing we should do over another, even when we need to do all the items on our now Success List. I want to add one word to our "Do It" List, and that word is *now!*

I think there's no greater place than right now to learn a term that is changing lives around the world. You ready for this? M.I.I.A. I can hear the clients of my 90-Day Challenge saying the answer: Massive Immediate Imperfect Action. You see the difference between those who know and those who go is found in execution. Winners find a way to make things happen, while others find an excuse to satisfy. Once I have my list identified, it's now time for **massive, immediate, imperfect action** that produces the desired results. Let's understand each word so you can operate full-throttle.

My wife and I had an awesome experience years ago when the Corvette came out with the Z51 engine. I'm not a sports fan, but my wife always loved the idea of having a sports car. Notice I said the idea of because you'll soon see she didn't like the reality of this type of car. I was working for AutoNation Chevrolet and had just received a promotion to become the General

Manager of AutoNation Toyota when we decided to reward ourselves by ordering a brand-new Corvette.

Now, up until this time, we'd purchased multiple cars, but neither one of us had ever *ordered* a car. Exciting times this was for the both of us. Tamara actually picked out everything. From the yellow exterior to the chrome wheels, she went through the ordering process with a good friend, Stephan Cooper. Finally, after waiting approximately three months, our car had arrived. We raced up to Dallas to pick it up, and after signing a few documents, it was time to drive the car off the showroom floor. Tamara did the honors, and then we switched seats for me to drive home in this powerful, sexy machine called a car.

"Slow down, you're going too fast."

Who says that when you're driving a real sports car? It was at this point that I realized no matter how much horsepower this car possessed, Tamara was going to drive this (list the stats of horsepower) the same way she did when she was in her 6- cylinder Lexus or even better, her 4-cylinder white Corolla which was the car she was driving when I first met her. I tell you that story to say, "You have massive inside of you, so stop playing scared. Push the gas down and open up."

I want you playing massively. In order to make it big, you have to play big. I've always been the adventurous risk-taker until I had the opportunity to take the biggest risk of my life when starting Assist U2 Win. I thought I was playing massive when I left AutoNation to start Assist U2 Win. I did what most of us do. I took a step, but only a baby step. Now, let me say baby steps in the right direction are still steps but, for me, I was leaving to start, not to false start. For about five months I attempted a new place of employment that gave me flexibility and thought I could do both. Maybe it could've worked, but for the type of person I am, it's all or nothing.

I remember meeting with my boss at the time and having to answer his questions with the right corporate answers, yet inside I was saying, "Walk. You know you don't want to be doing this." I was scared because I knew when I left, I would succeed. It wasn't failure that I was afraid of; I was afraid that my dream would really happen. It's a responsibility question that means there's no one to blame when it works or fails. Still, I needed some help taking the full step, and it came on a Friday when the company said, "We want to go a different direction." You don't realize how freeing that statement was. They asked me if I had anything to say, and I quickly said, "No; what's next?"

"Massive immediately" became a reality. I say go massive because it's the only way you'll get to the desired results. In my case, and the case of most, we get pushed towards massive. Massive looks differently at different times in our lives. For some writing a business plan, having an honest conversation with an individual, or doing a Facebook Live and telling people what you do could be your version of massive. Remember, massive is personal. It's relative to where you are, who you are, and what you are doing. No matter how you define it, know that you must face it in the journey of development and breakthrough. Oh, and know that once you face it, you'll have to face it again and again and again. Massive keeps showing up, but what it leaves behind is worth it. You have to go big because big produces the results you desire. Going small may get you started, but for most reading this book, small will not finish the job.

Now that we've conquered the word massive, the next word is immediate. I wish I could tell you that it gets easier as we progress, but I'd be lying to you. Immediate is so the voices inside won't talk you back to the bank. Immediate acknowledges now over later. Immediate understands and values time. When writing the teen collaboration, the words start now, arrive sooner leaped off the pages. Functioning with a sense of immediacy believes that today matters. Every day is a Winsday because each day I decide to get in action.

When we itemized our list, remember we added the word *now*. Do it *now!* That's the power of immediate. Immediate activates in faith while procrastination masks our fear—fear of being seen, fear of falling on our face, fear of being criticized, and fear of family rejection. Fear can keep you from, while faith can take you to. When I finally stepped into action, I realized the power of being creative. I create the reality I live in. I create through my choices and conversations the world I operate in every day. I make every day a

MAKE EVERY DAY A WINSDAY

Winsday. Massive *immediately* turns thoughts into things.

You're doing so well, let's tackle this next word—and forgive me if I stay here longer than you want, but this word is massive immediate *imperfect*. Let me talk about me right here. I'm not good enough, smart enough, pretty enough, or wise enough based on whose standards? This type of chatter is not admitted by most men, but let me be different and honest, since I'm out here. Confidence can mask insecurity, and only the individual understands this truth. To the world, I'm viewed as an online influencer. I have the outer personality of one who doesn't struggle as much as I know I struggle. Because, I can do through giftedness what others must work at, I can be overlooked from the individual who must work through this area of imperfection. Let me pull the cover back for a moment and tell you one story that can unmask all my issues at once:

It was in my thirties when I went to the orthodontist and said I wanted braces. Let's add to the pot of imperfection that we may say black don't crack, but when you're called blue black because of how dark you are, that's not a compliment. I just laughed when I typed that line, but there are years of dealing with implications and the negative side of these statements that aren't funny at all.

Okay, so now we have a dark-skinned, wide gap, stuttering boy whom I had to learn how to love. Yes; you hear me on TV, Facebook Live, and stages today, but it wasn't always this way. For years, I was pulled out of class to work on my speech. Don't feel sorry for me; we all have our issues that we must work through. Too many times, what we should have gotten over and through, we get stuck in the middle of—stuck in between potential and problems; stuck between destiny and history; stuck between positivity and negativity; or, stuck between limiting beliefs and unlimited opportunity. Our imperfections are the teacher that keeps humility as part of our lives. I realized that my imperfections aren't my reason to quit but are my reasons to run. It's in these places where those watching and following receive the most strength. It's in our humanity where I hope to do this as well.

So, how do we really deal with our issues? When I share this next statement, I'm not minimizing what we go through, but I am challenging you to see it from a different perspective. Our issues are our personal invitation for others to eliminate all excuses for why they can't. We don't all have the same abilities, but we all have common issues. Very few people, if they're honest with themselves, deal with some form of inadequacy at some point to their assignment. And for those who tell me they haven't, I am going to challenge them and ask if they've ever. If they haven't, I want to ask them are they playing as big as they can possibly play. I'm not using this to say the only metric is money; I'm using this to ask are you really playing full throttle. Who's driving this Corvette?

So, you may be wondering what to do with your issues. Let's start here:

1. Accept them as part of your makeup. They make you, you… as in unique. My story is built from my mess. My relatability comes from my vulnerability. No matter how the world views you, don't forget all of you. Facebook filters,

social media success, and vanity metrics shouldn't be how you grade your level of effectiveness. You are more than what they see and know.

2. Appreciate the value of your appraised assets. This term is used with homes, cars, diamonds, and other valuable items. We oftentimes diminish the value of items and label them as junk until junk has gone through the process of recycling. My mother's home is comprised of items she took from people who were through with them and, with vision and proper placement, she now uses them to decorate her home. If you could see her home, you would join those who share how her home looks like a model home. When you learn to appreciate the assets of your issues, the issues take on a new appraised value.

3. Avail them to those you encounter. I hid my story for 40 years of my life. I would only share the side that I thought you'd cheer and celebrate. Little did I know, people were reading right through me. They were waiting

for me to show "the real McCoy," as we state. When I finally received the courage to own and to share my dirt, I actually received more love and respect than hiding it from my tribe. I now make all my life available for those who need to learn a lesson. The lesson doesn't just come from theory or someone else's story; now, the lesson comes from both my pot of dirt and the planting of new seeds. I can speak from my pain without bleeding and encourage your potential and purpose.

The final word in the phrase is massive immediate imperfect *action*. It separates the talkers from the walkers. It separates the winners from the whiners. When you put the words together, it describes the difference between excellence and perfection. Perfectionists will not attempt or move forward until it's perfect; whereas, those who operate in excellence are always looking at ways to get better. One functions from a growth mindset, while the other functions from a limiting mindset.

I strongly believe we all have enough to get started, and those who start with what they have will be led to what they need. If you wait until you have all that you need to begin, you may never begin. It's easier to steer a moving vehicle than it is to move a parked car. Get into action; it creates a reaction.

Your movement produces momentum, and your momentum will change your moment. Every successful individual had to put feet to their faith. The only way to turn your thoughts into things is for you to put action to your thoughts. After we write them, meditate upon them, plan them, get counsel about them, black hat them, doubt them, we have to decide to do something about them called *action*. Our thoughts are in the refrigerator of our minds; action takes them out of the refrigerator and puts them into the microwave. From this place, we must remain consistently creative in order for what we start to finalize into our desired results.

The second response to items on our list is delegation. As you analyze your list, I believe there are one or two more items you think you need to do that you can actually delegate. I won't linger here, but let me give you a formula I use... If someone else can do the item 80% as effective as I can, I become willing to delegate. Don't fall into the adage of it's going to get done right, then I, myself, must do it. This will get you into trouble and will cause you to forget about empowering your people. Our job is to coach them to the place where they can do the work, and we are there to oversee and to provide specific assistance when needed.

Working in the dealership, I oftentimes said when it looks like I'm not doing too much, it means I've really done what I'm called to do. My job was to train my replacement. Oh, this thought is scary for many individuals, but for a visionary it should never bring fear. I will always have a job because there's creative power inside of me. When your vision ends, your control begins. With an increase of vision, I need quality empowered individuals around me to assist with the workload. My dream must attract a team, or I need to go back to sleep and don't wake up until I have a bigger vision for my life.

Now, on to the art of delegating versus dumping. The first thing I want to say is to make sure you delegate both the responsibility and the authority. Too often people get the task to do, but we don't give them the authority to carry it out. My delegated tasks should have proper guidelines, time expectations, reporting measurements, authority, and resources to fulfill the assignment. One of the most frustrating places to be in is to either be micromanaged around an area of expertise or given an assignment without the necessary resources to accomplish the task. The reason you are delegating to the individual is that they have displayed competence in this area. With delegation comes a deeper level of buy-in for the overall vision, the project, and belief in the relationship. Don't ruin this by dimming their greatness; instead, magnify them to the world. People love to be celebrated and acknowledged. It shows your belief and your value for who they are and what they contribute to the mission of the organization. Open acknowledgment is like oxygen to the soul. We all desire to add value and to be seen as valuable. Delegation is a direct result of one's gift being verified and trusted within the organization or team.

There are three main reasons why a leader chooses not to delegate. They are as follows:

1. Being busy makes a person feel that they are important.

2. The lack of confidence and trust in their associates keeps leaders from delegating.

3. The last reason why leaders choose to do it all themselves is control issues.

Some leaders desire to be busy over being productive. I tell people all the time that all activity doesn't lead to productivity. I learned this lesson as I was leading at Westway Ford. When I first got into the car business, I started off in sales. My income was determined by my production. The more I sold, the more I made—pretty good feeling to know that everyone around me could have struggled, and I still could've been successful. Well, this didn't last long because I was quickly promoted into management. It was in my first management position I realized the goal had to quickly change. It wasn't about just my personal production; it was way more about my ability to lead through people.

Leadership is a strong component of delegation. I had to gain the trust of the associates, and I had to develop them to be able to do, so that they wouldn't be dependent on what I did. Too often we need to feel a certain way, so we build an unhealthy structure that produces a poor culture for people's development, resulting in codependency and a lack of trust. Let's continue in this thought and learn the next lesson of delegation, which is every effort doesn't yield the same outcome.

Without going into much detail, you must measure what matters. Oftentimes, it's a lack of trust. To the control freak, we must address leaders who feel the need to do it all. How do you measure up? We talked earlier about the Pareto Principle, and I'd like to offer you a simple yet effective way of grading your activity. Each activity must stand alone and go through the following grading system.

MAKE EVERY DAY A WINSDAY

The 90 Day Challenge /Group Coaching™ ™ One on One Coaching ™ Business Coaching

	Daily Activity	Results Desired	Time Duration	Outcome Achieved
1				
2				
3				
4				
5				

When using this method, you must begin by listing out your daily activity. Let's do this together. Let's say you're in automotive sales, and one of your daily activities is to make outbound phone calls. We're going to:

1. **Write "outbound phone calls"** in our column that shows Daily Activity.

2. In the next column, **list our desired results** from our daily activity. Since I understand auto sales, I know we never just made calls to make calls. The result we were looking for when we made our phone calls was appointments to come see a car. So, one would list that under results desired.

3. In our next column, we would *write how long* we were going to perform this activity.

4. Finally, after performing the activity, we would need to ***write the outcome achieved*** from the activity.

Let's dive deeper into the details of why this is needed for every area of activity you state as part of your process for productivity.

1. Until you monitor and measure, you only assume you know what it takes to drive productivity.

2. Many of the actions we do daily either need us to adjust our results desired or need to be eliminated from our effort schedule. If it's not producing the desired result, we either have the wrong activity, or we need additional training and practice around the skill needed to perform the task.

If I saw a sales associate make 40+ calls per day, and day in and day out they never ended up with any appointments to sell cars, I knew I had a problem—possibly two. The first thing I would do was get closer to the associate and see if they were lying about making the calls. I had an easy way to find out. I would schedule a 2 x 2 meeting with my associate. Every time I did this, I was bound to find out all I needed to fix the situation. It was either the skill of the call, or the will of the caller. We would soon find out in our session.

A 2 x 2 meeting was my way of having a calling party with my associate. "Today, we're going to make calls together," is how I would begin. "I'm going to make two, and then you're going to make two." You know what I found out? I can hear you now. Yes; you're right. Most of the time, the associate just wasn't making their phone calls.

It was also here when I realized a valuable method that most fail to implement in our goal-setting efforts. I seem to name all of my findings, so I can remember and teach on them. I call this method **Making Decisions With My Desired Outcome In Mind**. It goes hand-in-hand with this principle and together can turn short-term intensity into long-term consistency.

I found out that when I would connect the activity to the outcome, and play it out in front of them, it would become apparent why I should be doing my what. Until my associate equated dollar signs with dialing, they would consistently be inconsistent. When you can start to think with the end in mind over every activity, it helps to produce the necessary disciplines needed to see results.

I think it's important for me to say, "Right behavior yields right results." In our generation of I want it right now, we must understand that our mindset for change happens before our methods change. There must be alignment and consistent action before the results show up in our lives. It's more like pumping water out of a well, rather than turning on the faucet in the kitchen. It takes time for the water to come up the pipes of the well, but when it begins to flow, you'd better have brought the right bucket to the well. This again is why we dealt with mindsets before methods. Your mindset is the bucket you bring to the well, and the methods are the effort of pumping that one does to produce the outcome they so desire.

Don't give up too soon. Keep pumping. I would send my associate back to their desk with a new sense of appreciation for the phones, and soon they would be coming back to me stating, "I have an appointment coming in tonight." I would high five them and say, "I know that's right." Remember, universal laws actively respond to your attitude, affirmations, and actions. All three must be in proper alignment.

Chapter 7

Excuses or Excuse Me

"You will find a way or find an excuse."

Sigh, "You know you were supposed to update Compass before going home. And, before you blurt out today's excuse, let me ask you a question, "Did you do it?"

Sometimes in management, you must alleviate the opportunity to hear the best storyteller tell their next excuse. Leading a team of sales associates, I have heard it all. It reminds me of the 4th grade teacher listening to why the paper just didn't get written. And for those who didn't know, I taught fourth grade for a short time in Duncanville Independent School System (DISD). It's these lies we tell ourselves that become the reason for our inability to make consistent progress. The lies come in different sentences, attacking different aspects of our lives. The result happens to be the same—no action and the hope of buying added time.

When you think about your goals and dreams, what really is a valid reason for not taking action? I'm not smart enough; they won't accept my idea; or, someone I respect doesn't want to invest in me. The list goes on and on. My question to you is what's your go-to when it comes to giving your reason (we won't call it an excuse) for your lack of progress? This question needs an answer because until you identify it, you can't confront it. You do know that what we're unwilling to confront will only serve as a blocker to our future desires, right? You and I can't change what we're unwilling to confront.

My limiting belief was a bad definition centered on the thought of my mistakes. Each major mistake was a lowering of self-value and worth which, in turn, meant I didn't deserve the great life I wanted from the beginning. I saw this as a bank account ledger. My good decisions were deposits, and my bad ones were withdrawals.

The major problem with this thought process is we don't give ourselves enough deposits, and we withdraw too much on the mistakes. Now, my dad attempted to teach me this lesson as a child. He would always keep a calm disposition—wearing about the same—no matter what took place. His highs never were too high, and his lows were never too low. Now fireball Derrick, on the other hand, was directly opposite. I was up, and I was way up. And when I was down, you just didn't want to be around.

I hid it quite well, but when I was in a funk, I was in one. The tragedy is this: I built an environment that didn't allow me to get into a funk. I struggled with being authentic and vulnerable. I wanted to do this, but I was fearful that if I did, you would judge what I showed, and you would go the other direction. My limiting belief was if they knew all about me, they wouldn't follow me. Isn't that crazy for the person who has shared the stories I've shared thus far? Oh, and it gets better. Wait until I share the story of confessing to my wife… Didn't I say you were going to have to wait?

This was truly the lie that ended up limiting my life and almost cost me my dream. Since you're reading this book and most of the time we read alone, please take the time to do inventory with yourself. If you don't unclog the drain, the water can't flow freely. There is a reason why you're not experiencing the level of breakthrough in your life that you're wanting, and most of the time it's because of some limiting belief that has crept in and set up residence. It's subtle how it happens, but when it gets in, it brings the entire family to the party. You wake up months and years later trying to figure out how you got here:

- Why do I think the way that I do?

- Why am I unwilling to take a risk?

- What keeps me from believing in my dream like I believe in the one's I see or hear on YouTube?

It's not ironic that you can have faith for someone else and struggle believing in yourself. I meditated on this thought for a while and concluded this: when you hear their story and dream, you normally don't filter it through any limiting beliefs because it's their dream and story. The difference with yours is you are telling you what you can do, but your story doesn't pass your security team that is standing between what's possible and what's blocking it, called your mindset or limiting belief.

At some point, you're going to have to receive some coaching around the topic of NLP (neuro-linguistic programming). My coach, Lisa Nichols, hosts breakout retreats where she walks people through exercises that help them reframe their thinking, so they can freely pursue their futures without the weights and limits of their past. Part of my self-help "junkie" library includes books that remind me about the power of my words and thoughts. I never understood the importance of energy and vibrations until I really began taking my coaching and speaking profession seriously. I spend countless research hours on these topics because I don't want any of those negative, limiting beliefs to creep back in and take up residence in my mind.

The moment you're willing to rid yourself of all excuses is when you'll be ready to tell the world, "Excuse me." This is said with a bit of an attitude. I'm talking about a "Bye, Felicia," or a "Listen, Linda," type of attitude. *"Excuse me,* I have places to go and people to see." "*Excuse me,* my dream has been on hold too long, and

I can't wait another day to get started." *"Excuse me,"* I have denied myself the privilege of loving myself, and from this day forward I will not beat myself up over your inability to see my worth and my value." Excuse me lets you tell yourself, "The rest of my life will be the best of my life." Joel Osteen said, "Every day is a Friday." I like to say, "Winsday can be every day."

So, how do you bring this level of confidence into your conversations? By doing the following:

1.   Recognize that the Creator doesn't make any junk. You are special and have a great purpose living on the inside of you. Shed the stinkin' thinking that somehow got attached to you and begin again speaking positive affirmations over your life.

2.   Remind yourself of the recycling process. Everything that could be junk can be recycled into something of value and significance. My mother is the master of this. When you walk through her home, you feel like you're in a model home. Don't let her be walking alongside you, she'll be giving you the backstories to how this and that came

about. Each story normally ends with some sale, some revamp, some I saw this and thought it could go with that. That's how life is when we allow our mess to become our message and our pain to become our platform. You didn't just go through it to go through it; you went through it to learn from it, in order to go back to it and help someone else who's in it.

3. Reframe your limiting belief into a power phrase that offers the possibility to become the very thing you state. My limiting belief was if they knew all about me, they wouldn't follow me. As I allowed Coach Lisa Nichols to walk me through this exercise, I ended up on the other side of the street where I began saying, "The best of me is all of me." This statement is needed at times when I'm facing rejection or thoughts that I'm not connecting with my audience. I have to remind myself that transparent and authentic is way better than impressive and perfect.

4. Release yourself from your past and give your future permission to live in your present. You have

to forgive yourself to free yourself. If we went to the state jail today and opened the cell doors, how many of the people locked up would just stand there when they could walk back into freedom? Will you please finish this story? Yes, yes, yes, and you know you're right. Your dream is waiting for you to exercise the power of choice to participate in your freedom. It will not automatically happen. You must give your future permission to live in your present with not another day living under the lies of yesterday, not another day waiting on someone to invest in what you haven't invested in yourself, and not another day wishing for someone to come to your rescue. Have enough power left to create the energy and momentum needed to take the first step out of your current situation. We can't run a mile without running a lap. We can't make a million dollars until we make a thousand. It's never too late to be what we might have been.

Can I please give you one more point? I was going to whether you said yes or no. It's my book, and I'm not sure when I'm writing the next one, so let's go there. Here it is:

5. Remove and Relocate to Remain Right. Okay, I said a lot, and, you already know this, but I need you to do this. Now that we've done all of this work on ourselves, there are things on the outside that can pull us back into our default. Remove the distractions. Let me say it better. Don't let the nouns disturb your verbs. I've had to remove people, relocate mentally and, for some, physically move, so that I could remain right in my actions.

"Excuse me or Excuses" is a matter of choice that will determine a life of design, or one of default. Which will you choose?

WINNING YOUR BEST LIFE

Finish the following sentence:

1. I am going to change what after reading this chapter..
2. The following excuses I have used no longer serve me because…

This chapter is my monthly "re-read and apply some more chapter." I'm not going to get in the way of your thoughts, so I'll ask one question: What are you going to do today with what you just read?

We've got this!

I'm a work in progress so give me grace, and I promise to do the same for you.

Chapter 8

When Your Thoughts Become Your Bully

"Whatever you think about, you'll bring about."

This is probably the single most important topic in the life of a leader. If you get this chapter, you will move from the brink of breakthrough to the driveway of your dreams. Close and closer are different because of the letter 'r'. Your success will be dependent upon the degree of your understanding of the topic of dominant desire. I'm going to make five power statements about dominant thought, and then I'm going to do my best to unpack them with a story. Here they are:

1. You are headed in the direction of your most dominant thought.

2. Your dominant thought should disturb your current default settings.

3. Your dominant thought determines the detailed directions, daily decisions, and your final destination.

4. You must acquire and keep a fire around your dominant thought.

5. Your dominant thought will dominate your life.

Each year for the last nine years, my wife and I have been on a cruise for one of our vacations. It is our preferred way of travel. So much to do, many things to see with our favorite being to people watch. Since you're not going to catch us in the pool, nor can I handle any more sun, we order the drink of the day and find a place of shade to relax and watch people. It's a site to see. We talk back and forth in code because one of us can't whisper and the other can't hear. Most of our conversation revolves around what people decided to bring on vacation. I often think to myself; *I know for sure they had something else they could've packed in their suitcase.* People are bold. The skinny, thick, or plus-sized individual can all be seen in something they should've kept back home. Well, that's my opinion, and they didn't ask me nor did I pay for their vacation, so I guess I should do me and allow them to do what they do. Oh! For the record, they are doing just that.

I tell this story because it illustrates our thought life. When one goes on vacation, they must pick out from all their clothes a few select items that they are going to pack and wear while on vacation. You can't take everything you own; you must choose which ones will go with you. When it comes to your dominant thought, the first thing you must know and own is **you have the power of choosing your dominant thought**.

The choice is yours! Not the people-watchers who don't know your name, didn't pay your fare, nor really care about what you have on. Their comments shouldn't be of concern to you. I must instate a familiar buttsism: *you will build what you birth, and you will drop what you adopt.* This dominant thought begins within, not without. In a society that social media influences so greatly, we find ourselves attempting at times to create a life that is measured by a standard of stuff that's just not real. You must shut off and silence the noise in order to become aware of who you are and what's important to you. The second point I notice is there are more clothes left at home than you bring on vacation, which means the other thoughts of your life can be left as well.

Is there a difference between your vacation thoughts and your home thoughts? When it comes to my dominant thoughts, most people's dreams and goals are like vacation wear:

- We only visit them every-so-often;
- They bring us joy;
- We know what they are; and,
- We travel there with them from time-to-time.

The reality of life is we live more often than not, thinking about our general day-to-day thoughts versus allowing our dreams and goals to become our dominant thoughts. If we could find a way to reverse this order, I believe we would begin to see life change right before our eyes. I must add another buttsism right here: Insanity and Destiny don't go together. Let that sit in as we turn the corner, and learn how to change, exchange, and rearrange our thought life. We must first change our thoughts. We must begin to think about what we're thinking about. This is work. It sounds easier than it is. This is a skill set that you will grow in, and the better you become, the greater the clarity and focus you will possess.

Allow me to get tactical and practical. Let's look at the steps I took in order to develop this necessary skill in my life. Here goes:

1. Schedule a reoccurring daily appointment with you and only you. This must happen daily. I like the mornings, but I will leave that totally up to you and your schedule.

2. Pick a place where you can silence the noises of life. No TV's, cell phones, iPads, or music (unless it's the meditation, thought-provoking music that stimulates the brain).

3. This appointment needs to be a minimum of 15 minutes per day. Quality is better than quantity, and consistency is critical.

4. Take the following items to the appointment: a pen, a pad, and you. ***For the first 30 days, please only bring a pen and a pad.*** No iPads, Surface Books, or note sections on the phones. They will become more of a distraction than they are of assistance. I don't want to know

what Facebook and Twitter thinks, we are after your thoughts. What's going on in your brain?

5. Listen to your thoughts (listener). What conversations are you having with yourself? Who's winning in the arena of your thought life? The seed you feed determines the harvest you receive. If you don't have my bookwork on *The DGCP Method for Winners,* I recommend you get a copy. In the final section, I walk you through 31 thought-starters for the day. I give you a quote and leave you some lines to journal. It's a great guide to begin practicing this principle.

6. The purpose of this appointment is to begin thinking about the outcomes, goals, dreams, and desires that lie within and what you would like to see manifested in your life. At Assist U2 Win, we call this defining what a win looks like for you. Without a scoreboard, how do you set targets? How do you know what to aim for? How do you know when to praise progress or to make tweaks and adjustments? Your

dominant thought should and will become your dream.

7. In the beginning you will need to bring a scratch pad as well. You will have things bombard your brain that you must jot down, so you don't forget and return to the assignment of thinking about what you're thinking about.

8. The more you do this exercise the better you will become. This is training and conditioning your mind. Soon you will be able to do this on the fly but, for now, let's stick to our daily 15-minute appointment.

9. We end each session by summarizing in our journal our thoughts and completing our affirmations for our life.

10. We create the future we want by our thoughts and words, followed by massive, immediate, and imperfect action.

I took the time to be detailed here because of the importance of forming and framing this dominant thought. Without it, you're merely existing; and, with it, you're an unstoppable force of nature. Without it, your best will only be mediocre; and, with it, the best version of you continues to evolve. Without it, the limits of your life have already been set; and, with it, you are unlimited in your ability and availability.

This method of movement is all about increasing and stretching our capacity. Our capacity must continue to increase in order for us to obtain the results of our opportunity. Opportunity always is greater than our capacity. Our dominant thoughts become the magnet that is known as the law of attraction.

I'm asking you to attract your dominant thought by subtracting all other thoughts.

WINNING YOUR BEST LIFE

I think, by now, you understand how important I believe this chapter is. So, why did I put it in a leadership book? Understand that in order to lead well, you must have a work ethic that is fueled by something internal, not external. So, what does this really look like in the life of a leader?

PART THREE:

MASTERY MAKEOVER

Repetition is the foundation of mastery.

Chapter 9

DON'T DISMISS THE 'MIS...

"Some games are won in overtime."

***Mistake #1**: Avoiding the signs that there were foundational problems.*

You don't just fall. You receive warnings throughout the process. Avoiding the signs only increases the crack. In my 20's, I was a star in the making in the church world. I knew the Bible and could see things others just couldn't; it is my gift from God. I am going to give you points throughout this story, the first being, every gift given must be guarded and governed. Operating in the gift, you can forget it is a gift and assume everything will be alright. How do I get to this point? Take a plant out of soil, a fish out of water, or a plug out of a socket, and you will soon find each of them loses their effectiveness and purpose due to their proximity to their source of survival. I unplugged from the Source and tried to operate the gift with no power. The greatest problem is you can function from this position for a temporary time, but you will soon shut off.

When your charisma takes the stage and your character gets left at home... a crash is about to occur. How thankful I am today for Pastor Eben Connor of Word of Truth Family Church. He did for me what many will not do, and that is caused me to deal with my decisions. I was on staff, and the day came when he asked me to do something different. That's a polite way of saying, you're fired.

Pastor Eben loved me then and still loves me now. I talk with him almost once a month, and I send members to his church as often as I can. The crash was my charisma may have gotten me there, but the lack of character development caused me to exit the stage. Lesson Learned: It's only a matter of time. I didn't end the statement on purpose because the ending is dependent upon your next move. For some it sends them into depression; for others it causes them to quit, while a select few use rejection as God's way of redirection.

In no way am I saying what I did was acceptable, but in every way, I am saying it is not the end of the world, unless you let it be the end of the world. For the next

MAKE EVERY DAY A WINSDAY

10 years, I learned how to succeed in spaces I never knew existed. You may be thinking about the money I made as a top sales associate who moved up the ranks fast and furiously or the General Manager position I received within three years of working with the largest retailer in America, AutoNation. Well, I'm speaking about character development. I took this failure in one degree, and let it become a reality check. I know I'm speaking to someone right now who needs to see the good in their bad situation. You need to see the tutor in the testing room. The outcome is defined by your outlook. I worked on the inner me, so the enemy could never win again.

Along the way I lost things, got a divorce, looked like a failure, had to start over, and decided the rest of my life would be the best of my life. Daily I work hard at co-parenting with my daughter's mother (the best mother for her I could ask for), rebuilding with my current wife and kids, and succeeding by discovering my sweet spot again. Failure can be a teacher or funeral director. You determine by your next move.

I used to hear people say all the time, "Make your next move your best move." I didn't understand that when I was younger, but I do now. My paradigm to problems is to find the side that's hidden to the natural eye. Gems are walked over every day. While you miss what looks like average, average keeps preparing for the person who knows what and who you are. Know your worth, and don't sell cheap.

Mistake #2*: Listening, believing, and needing the cheers of the crowd and their press clippings.*

In 1996 I was considered and named the 3rd Team All-State Basketball Player in the state of Texas. Looking back on it, this was a big accomplishment. Also looking back, they made a mistake. I wasn't that good at all. My setup determined my success. In 1994 I played with D'Juan Baker, probably the best basketball player Martin High School had at the time. In my opinion, he's the Michael Jordan of Martin High... still the best in my opinion. With respect to those Alumni who are reading the book, Willie Sublet may have given him a run for his money. Okay, back to the story.

It was the team I was on that made me, as an individual, look better than I actually was. This became evident when I was selected to play with the Top 60 players in the state of Texas. This game was held on the campus of Baylor University where we lost our only chance to go to state. Don't let me go too far there; it makes me sick to this day still.

Indulge me for a quick second. Friday night, we beat the #1 team in the state of Texas: Temple High. We were a game away from going to the state tournament, and all we had left was to play and beat Plano East. Who is this? When did Plano find them some basketball players? Baseball or golf, yes. Basketball? No way! Of course, overconfident and cocky will always fall prey to the hunter who is hungry. Yes; we lost by three and headed back home empty-handed. Lesson learned? Don't lose your focus when you're still in the fight. A knockdown doesn't become a knockout until the opponent stays down, and the match is declared over.

Waco was an eye-opener again because I found myself playing against guys who were serious about what I thought was just a game. Lesson learned: If you're going to do it, you better do it. From that point in my life, I began to take each task seriously. Those who know me know that I am competitive, and I want to win at everything. Don't believe every clap. There is a clap that is waiting for your failure. There is a clap that wants to see you quit. There is a press clipping that wants to record your failure as final.

Mistake #3: *Betting big on the wrong person.*

As previously stated, each year a select few friends and family members go to Las Vegas to watch the Super Bowl. Why Vegas? The energy of the city matches my energy. I know it's been named "Sin City." For my religious folks who are reading, go to the bathroom and look in the mirror. Whatever city you're living in can be called "Sin City." We are all sinners. I'm like Apostle Paul when he said, "I am Chief amongst sinners." The point being, we go to Vegas and watch the Super Bowl game. This time it was the Atlanta Falcons versus the New England Patriots (January 2019), and someone gave me money to take to Vegas and told me who they wanted me to place the wager on. For the record, the year before they were spot on, but this year was a different story. My "silent partner" missed every one of their bets. Lesson learned: Vegas was built on losers, not winners.

The even bigger lesson I learned was *don't bet big on someone else when you should bet big on you.* How did I put this in action? I got the courage to bet on me again. I realized how safe I was playing. Safe is not always bad, but it's not always good either. I was playing too safe. Go to work; get a check; buy some stuff; and do it over again. Oh no... this can't be the cycle of success. Is this what I was about wash, rinse, and repeat? This is the season in which I began to examine the pieces of my life. It was in the pieces of my life where the purpose of my life was rediscovered. I became aware, once again, of what was important to me.

I came back home from Las Vegas—with my new tattoo—and told my wife, "I'm going to get certified as a John Maxwell Coach." Now, I have every book he's written. I can almost quote every one of his points. I realized where my passion and love is. I love assisting people to win. Even though the registration had officially ended, when you want something bad enough, you find the courage to make the call in spite of what you see online. This is an example of taking massive immediate imperfect action. I figured out how to convince them to take my $5,995.00, and I headed to Orlando, Florida.

If I was telling this story in person, I would say, "It's about to get *gooder* up in here." At this point, I have in mind what I want to do with Assist U2 Win and actually just completed two live experiences. Add that to the pot of expenses because who pays to come and hear a guy who's been silent for years? So, basically, I paid to have an audience listen to me. LOL.

Though I've read all of his books and have been an Injoy Life Member for years, I'd never heard John Maxwell live by then. For the opening session on Sunday, I was like a little boy in a candy store. I was on the edge of my seat as John walked out to the stage with a Salt 'n Peppa song playing loudly, "What a man? What a man? What a man? What a mighty, mighty good man? Yes; he is."

In that moment I thought to myself, *this man is having the time of his life, and he's doing what he loves.* As I write this section, I can't help but smile right here. There's someone saying, "I want that feeling." I understand where you are because I myself felt the exact same way. (Now, I wasn't supposed to say this when for the past seven years, I'd made more money each year than I'd ever made, have a lovely home, drive nice cars, have a great wife and kids, and people around me seem to love me.) I'd learned the symbols of success will never satisfy nor compare to the substance of significance.

Listen, don't let social media fool you. Save photo, photo-bombing, crop, and editing have made the most desperate appear to be America's Most Wanted. While we lie on social media, the suicide rates are increasing, schools and churches are still being attacked, and poverty is steadily rising. We are also still under the systemic issues of governmental capitalism, and the rich are getting richer and not enough of the richer are purposely pouring back into the dying.

With John Maxwell operating in his giftedness and purpose, as I listened, I realized once and for all what it is I would do for the rest of my life. I finished the conference and was personally asked to stay over to a private session on Thursday. I called my wife and cleared it with my employer, then paid the price to change my ticket. Everything you need is not found on YouTube. I believe with all my heart there are things that are taught, but the best lessons are caught.

The expense of the experience is what took my good thought to a dominant desire. It was during my morning routine that I started solidifying my soul with the words of my favorite song, *You Will Win* by Jekalyn Carr. In this song the words kept ringing, "Everything attached to me wins." It was here where I became a multi-millionaire. It was here where I had more clients than time permitted. It was here where I spoke on stages all across the world. It was here where I became the CEO of my destiny.

What are you waiting on? When will you take control of your future and make the confession that your soul is waiting for? Let me tell you, once you do, the universe begins to align everything you need to begin and to become successful.

Chapter 10

Principled Plans Promote Predictable Outcomes

"Transferrable truths that work for whoever works them
are waiting on you to activate them."

Our paradigms are how we view the world in which we live. Our principles determine our actions. To live a predictable life, one must live a principled life. Principles are transferrable truths that work regardless of the people, place, or personal views about a situation. Principles are not partial. They don't show favoritism, nor do they ask our opinion before working. In an earlier chapter, I talked about the factors that shape our paradigm. Do you remember reading it's your experiences, environment, education, and exposure? For most individuals, these factors are the reason some are successful and the excuse why others are not.

What I love about these limiting beliefs are the stories we see on the news, read about in the papers, and even the ones we witness firsthand. It's the story of the underdog that gives us hope—that we really can control the outcome in most situations, based on the principles that are applied. It is true that some are naturally more inclined to use their skills in a way that enables or promotes success, but it still is true that if you learn the principles and apply them in your life, you too can see similar results.

With this knowledge, we can grow our future by following proven principles. You've heard it said, "Success leaves clues." This is true. Unfortunately, everyone is not looking at them like Peter Faulk did in each episode of Colombo. Too often we are mesmerized by the success of an individual that we don't look for the right things, nor do we ask the right questions. The quality of a conversation is found in the quality of the questions. Coaching has the ability to draw out of an individual, based on the depth of your desire to go deeper. We stay on the surface and miss the meaning of the individuals who pass through our lives.

I can recall when Bishop T.D. Jakes arrived in Dallas, TX. I was a young bible student studying ministry, and at the time I knew of most of the preachers in the city and, of course, the ones on national television. The city was in an uproar because the greatest orator of the gospel was coming to Dallas.

How funny and simple-minded these preachers were to think one man could come and take over the entire city. Take the population of Dallas and look at the size of the original Potter's House. If all the churchgoers in the city showed up on a Sunday, would they really fit within the walls of his congregation? We know the answer is no. Where should their attention have been? They should've been studying his marketing, his sermon preparation, and what he did in West Virginia to position himself as a major influencer. Studying the principles could've allowed them to learn and adapt, so they could adjust and have what he had, or at least similar results.

Even here we make the mistake of following his dressing style instead of extracting his principles. There's only going to be one Oprah, one George Bush, one Barack Obama, one Will Smith, one George Strait, one Jennifer Lopez, one Michael Phelps, one Tom Brady, one Steve Jobs, and only one you. You must remain original in your personality while being open to gleaning and implementing the principles of those who have had great successes before you.

I love how John Maxwell outlines the law of duplication. Anytime you see what you desire in someone else, no matter if you know them personally, or you're just a fan from afar, you are now looking at your new mentor. Too many people think we need to call them up and ask for a meeting. This would be nice, but it's just not possible in most cases. We have to learn by watching, implementing, failing, and starting the process over again until we master what we desire. Come on, you know how to do this! Every time I want to show my kids that I've got some dance moves, I turn on YouTube and hit play and pause until I can do the move well enough not to be laughed at when they see me showcase it. This is how you can begin learning from your new mentor.

I was amazed when I began listening to the comments of my first 90-Day DGCP graduates. I heard a little of me in them when they presented. Some of the lingo and definitions were the same. At first it made me chuckle, then I realized they were allowing the clues that I've been dropping to find their way into their toolbox, and they pulled them out when needed.

Don't try to reinvent every wheel. Instead of trying to make a manual car an automatic, have someone older than 35 teach you to drive it. Before you'll ever be a great leader, you must first become a great follower. The pattern is seen in your mentor and learned one principle at a time. You can learn to receive similar results by watching and applying what you see. At first it will be awkward due to a new method, a new approach, a new way of doing things. Just stick at it and watch how what starts off as uncomfortable soon becomes a normal way of doing business.

I did just mention the word uncomfortable. If you are unwilling to get out of your comfort zone, you just may miss your growth zone. Your tribe or company you associate with on a normal basis should provide a safe place for failure to occur. It's here, where you'll attempt new things that won't go right. It's here, where you'll find what works and what doesn't. It's here, where you'll understand that we beta now, so we can have better later.

I've mastered this place. When I launched Assist U2 Win, I failed at many things. I purchased programs, download apps, hired multiple web designers, launched programs with links that didn't work, and the list could go on and on. I invested my life's savings into my dream and realized that if I didn't attempt and only played safe, I would never experience the next level. You must be willing to trade in to trade up. Your decision to intentionally grow is needed when destiny serious.

Growth is optional, but it's always available. What I learned along the way is that you can't shrink your way into your dream; you must grow into it. Most dreams begin with words, not even complete thoughts. Inspiration comes in the form of jots. My version of journaling is jotting. Jotting is the exercise of putting down my thoughts on random legal pads. Where is the last thought? Trash cans hold millions of dollars that have come in the form of a jot. Too often we are looking for the entire blueprint to be written or downloaded when in actuality you only need a word to get going.

In 2019, during my New Year's Day Masterclass, I shared a lesson entitled: A Pen, A Pad, and A Plan. I would often hear people say or give me the reasons why they couldn't get started, and most of the reasons were valid. All of this was clicking for me until one day my best friend (Kelvin) brought over his wife (Sarah) and McKinley Joy (my god-daughter). I'm not sure of her exact age, but I will say she was just learning how to walk.

We know the first-place little walkers go in someone's home with stairs is to the stairs. I'm not sure what fascinates them about a staircase, but stairs and ceiling fans get the attention of toddlers fast. What I remember most about that day is McKinley Joy would go up the stairs and come back down the stairs again. At first, the parents tried to stop her. But they were at my house, and I'm kind of old school in my thinking.

I yelled out, "Leave that baby alone. She's just walking up the stairs."

Every dream—no matter how big the size—has steps. Too often we focus on the stage, or the end outcome, and we forget to focus on the step. What step are you on? What can you do, when accomplished, that will lead you to what you need to do next? Since I told you about Kelvin and his daughter, let me tell you what we would say to our sales teams.

You see, Kelvin and I worked together for over a decade building sales teams that could flat-out sell some cars. I've worked with many managers, but put us on a sales desk together, and it was like the Splash brothers of Golden State, or Kobe and Shaq days and, at times, we could even be compared to MJ and Scottie Pippen. I'm telling you; we were cold-blooded.

Every sales team across the world has some type of process. Our sales process went from Step 1: Meet and Greet, to Step 12: Delivery and Follow-Up. Two things you must pick up right here, and please don't miss it:

1. Your success is in the setup.
2. The most important step is the step you're on.

We repeatedly pounded these phrases into our teams. Why? If you don't handle Step 1 properly, you will never get to Step 2. There is someone reading this book, and you just received your #BOL. I'm sorry; that's another Lisa Nichols term I learned. It means Breakthrough Out Loud.

McKinley wanted to get to the top of the stairs, but if we watched her closely, she focused her entire attention on the step she was on. She may have wobbled at times, but she took a step, and although she may have slipped, she took it. Step-by-step she would go, and soon she would be at the top—back down to the bottom and, once again, she repeated the same process over and over until it was time to go home.

Okay! I got it, Coach Derrick. You just said to me, "Once my destination is set, the only thing I must focus on is the step I'm on, and that step will lead me to the next step, and step-by-step I will finally end up at my destination."

When I say I was cheering you on as you were reading that, I meant it. Internally, could you hear me saying, "Yes… yes… yep! Uhm hmmm, you got it?" One last word from Kelvin, and we'll end this chapter, "Now, go and be successful."

WINNING YOUR BEST LIFE

Give yourself time to see the results from the right behaviors. Too often I have quit something that was right because I didn't see the results soon enough. When making life changes, our commitment must be to the process. The by-product of working our process is the outcome we receive. This time go slower than the first time and listen to your listener (inner voice).

Chapter 11

AutoNation: THE BIG WIN

"Every win is not seen on the scoreboard."

There are two sides to every coin. I didn't tell you anything you don't already know. Unfortunately, most people only see the side that is shown. In sports, the umpire—before flipping the coin in the air—shows both sides of the coin and then proceeds to flip it. While the coin is in the air, the person who was designated as the home team must call heads or tails. You can't wait 'til it hits the ground to call; you must do it while it's spinning in the air. Carpe Diem is seizing the opportunity of a lifetime in the lifetime of the opportunity.

Jacob Bernoulli, a 17th-century Swiss mathematician, analyzed the statistics of random experiments with two possible outcomes. His trials became world-famous, mostly because there was nothing to do back then except math.

Since the first Super Bowl, heads have come up 25 times and tails 28. The winner of the Super Bowl has won the coin toss 24 times with heads coming up 12 times (half). Bernoulli would consider this a success since it proves the coin toss is random and won't always land the same way for each game.

I just believe we understand this as well. If we can make every day a Winsday, then we must do it on the days when the coin toss doesn't show us positive opportunities and instead lands on the side of adversity. Matter-of-fact, many times our greatest opportunities are disguised in our current adversity. This is where most get hung up on the hiccup. It's the same coin that was spinning in the air that could've landed on heads or landed on tails. Whichever side it lands on doesn't negate the fact that there's something on the other side. When your day begins, you must realize and come to grips with the fact that there will be both positive opportunities, as well as the possibilities inside of our adversity.

Why adversity? Great question, and I'm not the Creator, but I did learn something when I was experiencing a personal breakthrough. If I only acknowledge the power of my seed and don't appreciate the soil it would be planted in, I wouldn't experience the harvest from its growth. It wasn't just my successes that I need to be thankful for. I had to learn to appreciate, acknowledge, accept, and address my dirt more often. Your dirt is the mess that becomes your message, the pain that holds your purpose, and the clouds that hold the rain. Every farmer is appreciative of the rain if they've planted their seeds in the spring.

Don't despise your adversity. Adversity teaches creativity, determination, and exposes the strength of the soul. We often get so wrapped up in the drama that we miss out on the development. Wherever your attention will be, will be your intention. You have to begin to believe that adversity is carrying inside it your greatest opportunity.

THE DRIVEBY

In December of 2017, I saw a BMW 7-series pull into the lot of AutoNation Chevrolet and, from my seat, I knew who it was. It was the Market President. What does he want today? This is one of those positions that's a love-hate relationship. You love them because it's the boss of bosses but, on the other hand, you hate them because they always have something that's not going right. A quick text is sent to our management team informing them, "MP on property." This was our code, and everyone knew what to do. We weren't scared nor slacking, but we didn't want someone to get blindsided if they didn't have to.

Our Market President got out and headed to the entrance of our showroom. Always dressed to take a photo, the troops inside assume their working positions and act like they are diligently doing what they should be doing with him or without him entering the showroom. That's a whole other topic: why would you work to impress a person who's not buying a car from you today or, truth be told, ever from you? (Sorry, I had to say something. Work for your family, not for the man who doesn't know your name.)

Anyways, our Market President walked in and did what he always did, which was to shake each manager's hand and ask the question, "What do we have working? Are we set up for a day?" We'd answer his questions, and then he'd proceed to meet with our General Manager.

This day his meeting was quicker than normal, and as the doors slung open my name was called. I walked over and, in a simple conversation, I was asked to a luncheon. That wasn't strange because I ate with our General Manager at least three times per week, but today he wasn't coming. It was just our Market President and me.

We ate a Mexican restaurant not far from the store. As we ate, he shared how the corporate team had been watching me, and they were ready to give me my first shot as a General Manager. Now, this is what I've been working towards ever since I finished General Manager University. After attending this annual course, you work your butt off in order for them to come and give you a shot, which is what we call it.

Do you understand the term "a shot?" In sports the game is on the line, and the ball is put in play. Seconds are left on the clock, and somebody's got to take the shot. Ugggh! This brought me back to my sophomore year in high school at James Martin in Arlington,

Texas. We are making a run in the playoffs with Martin's best team ever. The only other team that would or could come close to this team was the Willie Sublett teams in the late 80's early 90's era.

We were in Waco, Texas, and that particular Friday night we played the game of our lives. I actually just got two rounds of chills even thinking about this moment in my life. It was Temple that was supposed to knock us out of the tournament and send us back home to Martin to prepare for our basketball banquet. Well, I wouldn't say it was an upset, but we did beat the #1 team in the state on the floor of the Baylor Bears.

We knew we had a game the next day, but there were still some celebrations in our hotel rooms that evening. I don't know this for a fact because I was the youngest on the team and the only Sophomore, so they shielded me from somethings, but I do know the great Willie Sublett was in attendance on a Baylor full-ride scholarship. Our high school All-American player, D'Juan Baker, knew Willie Sublett and allegedly went out to a college party that evening and didn't make it into the room until extremely late. Let's just say,

MAKE EVERY DAY A WINSDAY

D'Juan averaged 20 points per game and never—I mean ever—scored single digits until that night.

It was 11 seconds on the clock, and we were down by one to Plano East High School... only one game away from finally breaking the curse of making it to Austin, Texas for the State Tournament. Coach Husband drew up a play that had me penetrate to the side of D'Juan, finding an opportunity to get him the ball, so he could do what he does—and that's, take the shot.

D'Juan's shot would be one he'd made over and over in his lifetime. This was the shot you dreamt about while playing in the driveway on your first goal at your house. This shot was your version of winning the NBA finals, soon-to-be interviewed by Dick Vitale. You wanted the ball because getting the ball meant you had the opportunity. I received the shot that day from my Market President. "Derrick, we want you to take over AutoNation Toyota as GM at the start of the year."

Now, I must tell you that in order to appreciate the story, you need to know it came with the possibility of adversity being my greatest opportunity. While he was talking, I saw the coin flipping through the air:

opportunity. I was now a GM, adversity. Everyone before me had failed. You see, up until my arrival, the store hadn't had a month of profitability. This store drained the bank account of AutoNation monthly, losing over $300k not a year, but a month. Yes; I know. Do the math... That's $3.6 million, plus interest losses since we didn't have positive cash flow being generated.

The morale of the "troops" was down, and the only reason people kept coming was the guarantees they'd received. This was the set up I was given for the first chance at running a store with AutoNation. The Market President dropped me off after lunch, and he told me I had three days to let him know if I would accept this great opportunity. As soon as I got back into the store, I spoke to my General Manager who I respected and trusted with everything. He'd always helped me sort through opportunities and would add value without speaking about what may have been best for him; yet, he would give me his perspective of what he felt was best for the situation. He was hesitant to share his candid thoughts because, of course, he knew this was what I'd wanted.

MAKE EVERY DAY A WINSDAY

But, what happens when what you want comes in a package that is not so desirable? I wanted to be a GM, but who wanted to start in the dumps? I went home and this was the talk of conversation between my wife and myself. Now, if you know anything about my wife, she's a no-nonsense type of person, so once she knows what you're going to do, she doesn't like a lot of fluff to stay around the conversation.

Okay, the first night of thinking about it inspired me to write out my opening speech to the team. I printed all the numbers from the previous year; and, I ran numbers on each sales manager and every sales associate and put an order for 150 bracelets with a slogan that would be our rallying cry in my Amazon cart. "So, what do we need to talk about? You know you're going to do it. So, why not just make the call and do it?" my wife asked.

With only seven seconds on the clock, I passed the ball right in front of D'Juan and Lanny, and for the first time I can remember, neither one of our studs went after it; both assumed the other was going to get it. The ball bounced once, then twice, and next we heard a whistle. It was Plano East's ball with six seconds to play.

I was stunned. We were out of time outs, and all we could do was foul the second the ball was inbounded. We did, and they went down to make both free throws. We lost the game 50-47, and once again we had the long bus ride home. We blew our opportunity because no one took the shot. That feeling has stayed with me my entire life, and I promised myself—from then on—when put in those types of situations, I am going to take the shot myself.

My job as the point guard was to set up the person who would shoot the shot, but I had to do a better job of ensuring they were in position and were ready to shoot. When given the opportunity, I also had to be willing to take the shot in case they couldn't or just didn't.

Why do many in life fail to take the shot? Why have you foregone taking more risks? What are you afraid of? We could build a comprehensive list, but let's just stay around the obvious since we can't have a conversation to know your real reason. Most don't take the shot because they don't want to live with the outcome that they missed the last shot, and we lost because of it. I know you can't take that feeling away from an individual, but it's faulty, and we know it.

We had plenty of opportunities throughout the game to position ourselves better at the end. The last shot was just that—the last shot. My biggest complaint is we didn't give ourselves a chance to win. We didn't even get an attempt because the ball bounced out of bounds. If you don't get anything from this chapter, please get this: Be decisive. Make a decision and live with the outcome.

Yes; I woke up early that morning and made a phone call stating, "I accept the challenge, and thank you for the opportunity to be the GM of AutoNation Toyota." I'm not sure if I'd reached back into my high school days and remembered this story, but I do know my greatest opportunity came in the form of adversity. It looked different. It felt different. But, the outcome of taking the shot is why thousands listen to me from stages and is also one of the main reasons why I can offer business coaching today.

It was during this turnaround moment when I realized every positive story will not receive the same attention or appreciation it deserves, so you'd better learn how to celebrate your own success. I told you that when I arrived the store was losing on average $300k per month. I'm going to tell you the results, and you may take some time to learn the process.

Okay, during third month at the store, we lost $8. Now, I know if I was that close, and I was the comptroller, I would've found the money to make us positive, but that's okay. I was now too close not to break the barrier. In the month of April, we did it. The team finally did what no other team had done and that was make a profit at AutoNation Toyota. Later, camera crews arrived. AutoNation brought the Brinks truck to the lot, and we were also featured in *AutoNation News*. In addition, our picture was placed on the opening webpage for our company portal. Beyond that nothing else was done. Matter-of-fact, beyond a visit from our Market President, they didn't do a damn thing. Sorry, I had to say it exactly how I felt when it happened.

Are you kidding me? This team had busted their tails morning and night, endured all the ridicule of the past, and had figured out how to squeeze out a profit from a store that was losing $300k per month. And, that as it. We were recognized, but we were not celebrated. So, when they won't throw you a party, you just have to throw yourself one. We partnered with my friends from junior high school and had a day where we had live music, hotdogs, and we celebrated our own success. Don't wait for others; set your goals, accomplish your goals, and plan your own party.

It did bother me, and I believe it was here when I allowed the seed to enter in and the shift started to happen. When you work very hard for something and the reward isn't there, you quickly question if your ladder is up against the wrong wall? I am not saying we should've gone on a month's vacation, but something for a job well-done after no one in my market had ever done it would've added fuel to the journey. Isn't it something when we give more attention to drama than we do to success? I'm not vindictive by default, but I know how to get one's attention, and I'm willing to do it. For me principles over paycheck are how I've always operated.

Quick story about when I was a Finance Manager, and the Director decided he forgot who he was. He was upset for something, and he paraded into my office and straight-up thought he could disrespect me. Oh! I didn't play that in the business, and I didn't accept the statement that this is just what we do. You might do this or that to everyone else, but I respect me, so you will respect me too. I know the value I walked in here with, and I know it's wanted elsewhere.

So, I quickly interrupted him and said, "You need to change your tone, or you can stop talking to me." He held a higher title; I held a higher place of value with the company. We both decided that talking to each other wasn't the best option that day, and I went to another area of the store and did something else. Before I left, I told him I wouldn't sell another service contract until he got himself together and apologized for his behavior. He threatened me and reminded me that my money would suffer. I told him I would rather not make anything this month to prove to him I'm serious. Yes; my money would suffer, but so would his. I knew I could outlast him.

It only took three days of him seeing I was serious until he came in and closed the door. We had a grown man conversation, and we got everything we needed on the table and gave and accepted apologies and our work-life went back to normal. Well, this didn't happen quite the same with my corporate team. The month of April ended, and I started to get these e-mails asking could I get to $25k per month. It wasn't the number that scared me; it was the approach and words that followed. Hindsight is 20/20. They wanted me to give these projections, then sign my name as if to say this was now the expectation. Four months ago, they'd basically had to beg someone to come and take the job. Now, they'd found someone who got the job done, and they responded by saying the bar has been too low the whole time.

The writing was on the wall, and it didn't sit well with me. You see, I never fit the traditional car guy image. I'm wasn't into fancy suits, Rolex watches, and Gucci shoes. I was your normal Polo-wearing, people-loving, let's-get-the-job-done, so I could go home type of person. Matter-of-fact, I wasn't motivated the same way they were, and when I found out I did all that I did, and those before me did worse but made more, the seed that entered received water plus growth enhancer.

You do realize some opportunities are to teach you something about yourself that you'll need at a later time in your life, right? When I look back on those days, I now can draw from the immediate success and find strength in adverse situations. With little to no budget, troops that didn't want to be there, and failure all around me, I was able to find a vision, communicate the vision, and strategize around the vision to produce a profitable market share. I made the manufacturer mad for the moment, but they too came around and pledged to assist in the building of a brand new building.

Since this book isn't about my car days, let me tell you they built a building that I never got to occupy, and I got asked to leave after having the most success. I didn't understand then what I know now, and that is while I was grinding to sell more, serve more, and become more, they were negotiating with another buyer the entire time. The stock value of our store went up each month the team produced more and more stability. When they sold the store, every employee who was there was now the employee of the new owner. I didn't know slavery still existed, but corporate slavery does still exist. Here's what I was supposed to learn for my legacy:

1. Focus on your development, and your future will be secure.

2. Negotiate from a position of value and worth, not one of fear.

3. What you can do for them, you can do for yourself.

I could list many more, but I want to stop right here. I started to reset my value and realized I was sitting at the right table; I was just in the wrong seat. Too often we are at the table where they are telling us what we have to do, versus being at the brainstorming sessions talking about what we could potentially do in the future. We need to be in the decision room, not just the execution room.

When your value of yourself rises, you see from a new set of lenses. Respect is given and must be maintained through your actions and integrity. If one doesn't deserve it any longer, please don't fool yourself because you think you need them to survive. There's a difference between the source and the resource. Your job should always be a resource; it is never the source. When your resource needs to change, you must be willing to make one.

Also, don't get stuck and forget to scale. No matter what level you climb to, there will always be tradeoffs from one level to the next. Many times, during the tradeoffs, you will take a dip before you enter the rise. The dip is like jumping on a trampoline. If you can't make the trampoline go down, the trampoline doesn't feel the tension needed to make you rise.

Coach Lisa Nichols says all the time, "I'm okay with stretching you; I don't want to stress you." Are you being stretched in every area of your life? What are you avoiding that you need to deal with? What can you do to set yourself up better? Let me be clear, sometimes self-help books position the reader to think we want everyone to leave their jobs and start their own business. That's not the case at all. I want you to extract the principles of being all you can be in the place you're supposed to be. You can be at home or in Corporate America; regardless, you need to be stretched in order to grow. Very few individuals shrink their way into success. Most of the time, it takes intentional growth. I'm on purpose for purpose doing everything that I do.

When I now look back on my days at AutoNation Toyota, I pull from the strengths and not from my pain. Honestly, these were the best times in the midst of the worst of times. I just didn't get it then, but I do now. If I would've stayed on the trajectory path of growth with them, I would've never started Assist U2 Win, and I would've never wrote this book. It really is true that what doesn't kill you can build you.

WINNING YOUR BEST LIFE

Don't allow the good that happens from a bad place make you bitter when you should be better. Reflect on a thought that you may have once labeled a bad situation. What did it teach you? Are you using the lessons from your experience today? Who did you become as a result of this experience? Who can you help, or how does it help you in your current opportunity? Don't throw away the baby with the bath water. Take some time in reflection before moving forward into action.

Chapter 12

WINNER'S CIRCLE

"Multiple beginning points with no sight of an ending point."

The life cycle of a client within the connecting place for winners has only a known entry point with no sight of an ending point. In strong business communities that understand collaboration with a purpose, each entity is connected to add value when the time is called upon for the clients within the community. As a business leader, I am responsible for attracting new clients into our ecosystem. This model works perfectly when all parties are growing and doing business with integrity and excellence.

Oftentimes, businesses get a bad rap because of something someone within the organization has done. I understand this will happen, and when it does, it can impact the entire community. I don't like to label businesses. I would rather label an individual. You see, the integrity of the individual determines the integrity of the business. Businesses function with people who develop processes and sell products. It's the people whom we should focus on more than any other part of this equation. People's development will determine business projections. When an individual stops growing, soon the business will follow. This is why we should all be committed to personal development. The more I grow, the more it grows.

Now, back to the life cycle of a client. When we understand that value is performed, then passed to what the client needs next, clients appreciate value, and they never feel that they are being sold something. Our business model functions from the Radical Candor philosophy that states, "We personally care about each client, and we can also challenge directly each of our colleagues with whom we do business."

It is not my responsibility, nor my obligation, to refer my clients to someone else's business, but it's nice to have a community of professionals who all work from a similar place of excellence. This keeps the money within the circle, but most importantly, it adds value to the client based on their needs and wants, not the business leader's. Unselfish leaders can do and share business with others, while "in it for me only" individuals' function with a catch and release model. They catch business, benefit from the client, and then release them back into the world to find what they need next. This is not truly serving our clients. I believe we should create win-win scenarios and forward think with them, connecting them to their next answer. This model is a unique and rare find in our society.

How do you create communities that understand the life cycle model? It begins with the end in mind. You must be willing to think client first, not your business and what's in it for you. Every time you encounter a client, you must think "what do they need, and what's the best way to serve them today?" When we start to adopt this philosophy, we are the beginning point some days and the final leg in the race on others. So, whether you're passing the baton or receiving the baton, it is your commitment to the client that must remain the main thing.

If the circle is not broken, every business will benefit at some point. Yes; you need business today, and your direct marketing will normally attract people who need your services. You must also adopt another's focused model, so that the transaction is only the beginning and not the end. We are always looking for additional ways to serve our clients, so let's have some options. See below:

1. **Operate your business with integrity and excellence.** You will attract who you are not just what you desire. The community begins with the individual. Decide today that your business will be everything it's called to be. Don't shortcut your process. Shortcuts equal pay cuts in the end.

   All through my sales career, I challenged my team to follow our process and road map for sales. Each step in the process is important. Matter-of-fact, the most important step in the process is the step you're currently on. If I don't fulfill this step with precision and excellence, I may never receive admittance to the next step in the process. You see, great closers are first great openers. If your backyard gate isn't open, you don't and never will be able to close it. I'll expound more later, but the point you need to receive here is you have one shot to deliver an experience that is either desired or rejected.

I spend a lot of my time asking myself, "What do I do that is memorable"? If we're not leaving an indelible mark on our clients, they will not become raving fans. ***There should be excellence in everything***. Notice, I didn't use the word perfection, I used the word excellence. The difference between perfection and excellence is one desires to wait until everything is perfect to begin, while the latter begins with their best version and continually gets better every day.

I attended Amp Fitness for about three months. This is a CrossFit Bootcamp style of gym for fat folks. I was right at home, and it was actually the best style for me. Loud music playing, an instructor who was on 10 at 5:00 am in the morning, and a group of desperate, yet committed individuals who all desired something different from our bodies. This represents the recipe for transformation.

After being led through an intense hour workout, I would be drenched in sweat, ready to pass out, and we would end by breaking it down like I was playing high school basketball all over. "How you feel?" "Fired Up." We would chant for about 30 seconds, and then end with these words: Amp Fitness, we get better every day. If this could be our motto in life, personal development, business objectives, relationships, and all other places that need the best version of ourselves, wouldn't we be okay… if we really focused on getting better every day?

What if we really had the challenging conversations about the places we see—where we're just doing enough to get by—and we really put the attention and resources needed to improve our processes where they are needed? How would our clients feel? Would loyalty look different? Would our bounce rate decline? Would our referral process increase? To what percent?

Think of the money we could save if every client turned into three future clients. If you don't see each client as a seed leading you to future business opportunities, then you're not functioning within the life cycle we explained earlier. Your business will increase at the rate of the value you deliver.

2. ***Go the extra mile to separate yourself from the pack.*** Now that you're functioning in a place of excellence, I want to challenge you to go the extra mile. What do you do with them or for them that separates, or differentiates, you from your competitor?

    With the increase of target marketing, you do know that loyalty is declining at a rapid pace, right? Clients are no longer loyal to the person; they are becoming loyal to the deal. Why is that? We rarely talk anymore because people prefer to text. How impersonal can business become when the information can be accessed by a few clicks versus a direct personal call?

The decline of human interaction is being challenged every day when it comes to scaling a business. How much will the client allow me to automate? This question is the one that replaces human touch and interaction. The more I can remove a human, the less I pay for labor. In the midst of most sales processes, the need for human interaction is still there. It is why effective communication is the single most important trait an individual can possess.

We are all speakers, and we must all learn how to improve if we are going to last. When I think about going the extra mile, I think about being a digital disruptor. Why will they stop and choose me over the other 1,000 brands that are competing for their attention, time, and resources? If you're not the biggest on the block, you must be the best at something the big folks are unwilling to do. What's your secret sauce? Define it and deliver it better than anyone else.

That last sentence is what makes Chick-Fil-A have lines wrapped around the building at lunch. We go because of their impeccable service and their willingness to improve their processes to remain relevant and effective in the fast-food industry. Go to a Chick-Fil-A during lunchtime, and you will experience outside workers taking your orders, allowing the line to flow expeditiously and effectively. Just because it's slamming doesn't mean the service is compromised. I still receive my food hot, and my thank you/my pleasure is never forgotten. You can't control the rain or the lines, but you can control the implementation of your training modules. They are serious about their communication with their clients, and we say thank you by forming the lines around the building.

Do you have this level of service? Why are your clients returning? Where do you return to and why? For those of you who don't have a business, but value and appreciate great customer service, maybe you can slow down this weekend and write a review. People use reviews in their decision-making process. The more positive reviews a company receives can assist them in acquiring new business or keeping the business they have.

3. ***Connect with others who are doing the same thing.*** Birds of a feather flock together, most of the time. I had to put that in there because we only know what others are willing to show, or what we are able to see.

Bad assumptions are normally based upon limited information. I'm not asking you to be a detective with your connections. I am asking you to do business with people who exhibit the same qualities as you do. It's just easier to refer and receive business from individuals who flow and function similarly. The easy tale of how one will be treated is in how you are treated and in how they communicate about the way they treat their clients. One open-ended question will turn the faucet on, and they will tell it all, so be prepared to listen. Take mental notes and begin to see if what they say is also what they do. Now, we are not looking for perfection, but you should see consistency around their statements. We all have one-off's, and there's always the exception to every rule, but you're looking for trends. Data shows trends.

A word of caution to the life cycle community, don't keep score when it comes to referrals. First, your business may not be desirable, and the need to sustain it may not be in the volume of leads. Keeping score means one team wins, and one team loses. This is a sure way to break up communities and give way for the seed of bitterness to be deposited within your heart. Once this happens, you might as well leave and not destroy the community. Whoever allows the seed to enter, it's just a matter of time until the bomb explodes. This is shown in subtle statements, social media posts, the building of side groups, and in the end the defamation of someone's character.

Groups that confront the little weed head-on will eliminate the growth and destruction later. Don't avoid the droppings. Deal with it with the heart to restore but have the willingness to remove anyone if the behavior persists. You must protect and guard these communities. Again, they are rare and hard to find, but when they are established and are functioning, they are a machine of business momentum.

WINNING YOUR BEST LIFE

This is one of my favorite new thoughts that I am currently developing within Assist U2 Win. I challenge you to find a networking group where you can add and receive value. Find out what others offer and need. When you find ways to serve others, the boomerang effect always finds its way back to you and your business. Keep your heart right when assisting others, and you will always have people wanting and willing to assist you.

Chapter 13

Don't Forget You, Too

"You're worthy to be the priority."

The teacher often focuses entirely on the student and their development, which they can get addicted to helping, and forget that they too need help. It's hard for me to respect those who know what to do, can say what's needed, but for some reason or another, are unwilling to do it themselves. I'm in the coaching and speaking business. I love coaching individuals. I have clients that pay me to coach them for a variety of reasons, and I'm blessed. I am now at a point where I won't take every client that's willing to pay. Not because I'm too good or my fees are too high, but maybe it's because we're not the right fit, or my focus and expertise are not what they need.

I believe in coaching so much that I myself have coaches. My two main coaches are John Maxwell and Lisa Nichols. John has coached me for years. Through his tape club called Injoy, his books, his seminars, and his latest IMC Conference, which certifies speakers and coaches. His ability to shed information and nuggets on leadership has led me to top positions within my corporate career.

As of late, Coach Lisa Nichols has taken over the reins for my development. The proximity and intensity she has brought into our sessions have brought internal healing and immediate success within my coaching business. You have to know what you need, and you have to know who you receive from. Her style, her candidness and, most importantly, her investment in me was all I needed to begin making the investment in her. For Lisa to give me her time the way she does is priceless.

Tell me how much is freedom worth to you? Before you answer, please think of people who are bound. You can go as far back as slavery—Dr. Martin Luther King, Jr. in and out of jails because of the civil rights movement—or, you can simply think of being held captive to a limiting belief. When I met Coach Lisa some might have said, "Derrick, you know you're the next..."

Truth be told, I got sick of hearing that statement because the next meant I'm still not up. The longer you have to wait, the more you have time to think. What if? Will I? When? Are you sure? The list goes on and on. What lies between right now and next up most of the time is you. It's not always the need to fix the gift; you may have to do what I did and fix the box that's housing the gift.

I met Coach Lisa live in Arlington, Texas at my good friends' Tommy Jones and Nicki Ferrell's event, A Glimpse at Greatness. Tommy and I spent plenty of mornings encouraging each other, as we both are shifting careers from corporate to calling. Twenty years ago, Tommy Jones told me, "Your money is in your mouth." Twenty years later, he invited me to be his lead-off speaker at the biggest event Arlington has seen in years: A Glimpse at Greatness.

Friday night during the VIP dinner, over 300 individuals are dressed up in their Sunday best and all are there to see Coach Lisa Nichols. Prior to the event, Tommy called and gave me last-minute instructions. "D, I need you to set up the step and repeat banner, ensure the band is in the right spot, and please do a quick walk through the room. You know what to look for; act like this is a revival, and Bishop is coming." (He said that because we grew up in the church running events with our teams, and we had access to the who's who of the church world.)

Some just missed the first lesson. You can't get so big-headed that you're not willing to serve. Your stage is special because of the work you do before the audience arrives. Don't get beside yourself and think that it's the knowledge you bring as to why people want you or choose to request you. Your heart is seen behind the scenes, not on the stage.

So, as the night rolls on, Lisa did what she does. She delivered a challenging message to the game-changers, and then went back to working the room. Oh, I didn't tell you that my seat was in the back of the room at table 24. Now, I was a main stage speaker tomorrow, and I didn't have a seat with the speakers? No, I sat with my wife and a group of ladies. One of the most special moments was when a lady from All-State saw Lisa coming and said, "I'm going to get a picture with her." She got her picture and sat back down and said, "I touched her, and she gave me a hug." As tears rolled down her face, I realized the depth of connecting with people is life-altering.

The entire night, I didn't stop watching Coach and her every move. By the way, at this point, she wasn't my coach, and I wasn't her student. I should've been in the photo lines getting me some social media clips to use for my website and promo materials, but this night was not about that at all. I shook hands with those I knew, made small talk, and kept my eyes on Coach.

The night ended, and I went back into the empty room to take down the banner as I was instructed and put it in the trunk of my car. Then, the wife and I headed back home. In the car my wife asked, "What did Lisa say to you, tonight?" I said, "Absolutely nothing." She said, "Derrick, I noticed that as well. Why didn't you approach her like everyone else?" I said, "I did." She said, "No, you didn't." I said, "Honey, I received what I came for. I didn't want to get in the way of people who needed this moment. Mine will come later."

I chose that night to not approach her. Not because she wouldn't have taken the picture or said hello, but because that night I was given access to see my future in operation. I watched how Lisa smiled, what she said, where she sat, when she sat, and listened to what she said. Sometimes the greatest lessons come through watching and not talking. I like to say it like this, "Some lessons are taught, while others are caught." Oh, did I catch a lot that evening!

The next day was the big day. It started early for me because I had the step and repeat banner, and it needed to be set up before the kids arrived for the second day of festivities, a youth empowerment event. I packed the car and left the house. It was raining cats and dogs that day, but we pushed on and had a great "Aha" Experience.

The time finally came for the main stage speakers to share their messages. Constance Carter was on the mic when Lisa Nichols was brought in through one of the side doors. There was only one seat left on the front row, and guess what… yes, it was right next to me. I extended my hand and whispered, "Hi, my name is

Derrick Butts. It's so nice to meet you." She said, "Hi, I've heard about you, and it's good to meet you as well." I asked if we could take a selfie, and she said of course. Snap! Snap! And, at that moment, I was being called to the stage because I was the lead-off speaker. I spoke. Sat back down, and she leaned over and said, "Quite impressive."

The next three speakers spoke and did a fabulous job, and now Coach closed us out. She shared her story and led us into motivational moments and transformational turning points. Before she ended her message, she looked at the speakers and extended a VIP invitation to join her on her campus in San Diego, CA later that month. I immediately checked my schedule and thought *I have to clear the calendar to be in this room; I haven't been moved by a speaker like this in a long time.*

Tommy and I actually coordinated travel arrangements and took an early flight out to San Diego. We went straight into a session in progress. Matt Gil was leading us through a pause and play exercise that helps you stop those negative thoughts, giving way for the positive ones to live. He concluded by challenging us to play big throughout the entire conference.

On day one, I got called out of a crowd of 250 VIP's, and Lisa Nichols straight out busts me down after the crowd cheers my performance to the request that was asked of me. This is the moment I knew she would move from Lisa Nichols to Coach Lisa. I needed someone greater than myself to recognize that half-ass playing is no longer acceptable. There's not another word that could have got that point out.

My good has been labeled as great by a lot of people with the exception of my inner-self and my business bank account. If I was really that great, then why was I not that great? In case you forgot, I can struggle with pride. I have a lot of self- confidence, and I think I can hold my own. So, I'm holding my own but, in actuality, I'm holding me back. Coach called me out, and the entire conference referenced me from the stage, yet busted me up along the way.

You see, if you don't focus on what others can't see, you will never be seen by others. My problem wasn't my gift. My problem was my mindset... Not Mister

Positivity, right? I could talk you through your mindset because I know content, and I know people. I could sell you on what to do, but I couldn't sell myself on my value. I had countless individuals give me the medicine; yet, it was not taken because I couldn't connect to my calling. Coach Lisa was walking out what I know I'm called to do and to hear it from her sealed the deal.

I don't want you to make this mistake in building your dream. Listen and please don't overlook the next few lines: If personal development is not part of your step-by-step plan of action, your business will hit a roadblock. You can't build it without building you. Matter-of-fact, you will hinder it more than anyone else can help it.

When I focused on the inner me, the outer me was released to be versus to do. I moved in an instant from impressive to impactful, from attempting to be perfect to accepting being authentic. Der-rick was left in San Diego, and Derrick Lee Butts came home. Part of me arrived, and all of me returned. I learned at that VIP experience that the best of me is all of me. As I'm writing, I'm owning my life. I know the methodology of the DGCP Method for Winners, and now I can connect with my life. Content without connecting is like eating food with no salt. It's bland and only a select few have the desired taste for that type of eating.

You are too valuable of a seed not to plant yourself in development. Somethings need to be uprooted while other things need to be watered and exposed to the right sunlight. I, as a coach, vowed to move up the layers of coaching because I know you can only withdraw after you deposit within. Our tribe has room for people like me and you to be real, transparent, and vulnerable leading us to the ultimate goal of developing our voice of authenticity.

WINNING YOUR BEST LIFE

Take time to invest in yourself. Stephen Covey says, "Sharpen the saw." You are the saw. Make sure you are not so busy doing that you forget to check on your blade. Effectiveness comes when you are doing what you are called to do from a full plate and not an empty tank. The encourager needs encouragement.

Answer these sentences:

1. Who do you receive from?
2. Who can tell when you're running low and you need a break?

Make sure these individuals are close enough to you so they can see the warning signs before the breakdown. Please remember, the bigger you play, the bigger the breakdown.

CHAPTER 14

ACTIVATE YOUR 'AHA'

"Life only rewards your actions, not your good
intentions."

The decision to make every day a Winsday begins and ends with you. By now, you realize that my life isn't anywhere close to perfect and, truth be told, no one's life that I know is even close to perfect. Since it doesn't seem like perfect is possible, I've committed to controlling my mindset, living as best as I can by principles and methods, and doing it daily until I've developed a sense of self-mastery. Pastor Eben Conner says, "To live a predictable life, one must live a principled life." Now, some days are easier and better than others, but every day can be and is a Winsday.

For the rest of this chapter, I'm going to walk you through a normal day of my life. I'll stop throughout, highlighting and pointing out some of the methods I implement. My hope is for you to hear one or two "Aha's" that, once applied, can change your right now. My daily routine is not recommended for you to follow; it's just an example of what it's like to begin living on purpose *for purpose*. Once again, this list is not the end all be all list, but it is some of our top methods that I coach my clients around, and over time I've found these to be helpful in designing the life I love. If you're ready, let's go ahead and get started—from my waking moments to my laying down.

Wake Up

I'm an early riser—I mean *early* riser. My wife would say I only sleep a solid 4-5 hours per night, which I'm actually not proud of. I'm working on this area of my life because my effectiveness will not be sustained if I don't figure this out. I hate to say I have high blood pressure, and my poor sleeping habits don't help the cause. There's someone reading this book right now who will be bold enough to contact me and offer me some coaching around this topic. I'm an easy close, so please reach out.

4:30 am is my get out of bed time. If I'm tired, I'll lay there until 5:00 am. The first principle I will share is the Bookend Principle. We have two bookends, the first and last 30 minutes to an hour of each day, which hold everything in the middle of our day together. Most individuals prefer one over the other. I rarely see someone who functions just as good in the morning as they do in the evening. As you can see, I function better around the morning bookend. I choose to wake up earlier than anyone else in my home, which helps me to eliminate most distractions. I have a handful of individuals who are in my inner-circle who, from-time-to-time, may send a text, but for the most part, no one is posting, e-mails aren't arriving, and text messages are barely buzzing, which allows this time to be my uninterrupted alone time. Since this is my best energy, most focused, and clearest of thoughts time, I spend this time in prayer and meditation, bible reading, journaling, writing, and reading self-development, or other growth materials. Also, I attempt to complete my most challenging projects, or the ones I know I need heavy focus and individual attention for. The reason this works is that focused energy and efforts produce major results. Our hustle and bustle world seems to require and reward those who can multi-task, even though studies have proven greater effectiveness is found when individuals focus on one project at a time. I am learning day by day how to become creatively consistent around my core competencies, which yield me maximum returns.

6:00 am is when my first coaching calls begin. My clients must work when I function best, so we begin as early as possible. I've been asked over time to begin earlier than 6:00 am, and I've been tempted to say yes. What keeps me from doing so is the thought that my blade will become dull, and I'll lose my superpower. My superpower lies in my ability to hear ideas and immediately have multiple suggestions, thoughts, or ways to enhance my client's world. My thoughts are sparks that produce the flame. So, If I forfeit the connecting moments where I receive my power charge and peer-to-peer accountability, I will soon wear down and lose my edge for creativity and strategy. This will result in my clients' growth declining, which will leave them no other choice than to start searching for another solution to meet their coaching needs. I really don't think people will give too many two-week notices, but changing their credit card information or refusing to schedule coaching calls is a pretty good indicator.

I know I'm speaking about my routine, but I must add some commentary for my scaling entrepreneur. Growing your business too fast can cost you your business sooner than you know. The decline of the business begins the moment you leave the principles that you started growing your business. You don't have to do the same things, but you must remain committed to the principles of development and structure. It's not to say you won't tweak and make adjustments along the way, but I can't forfeit the proven structure for the attractive dollar. Long-term consistency always outlasts short-term intensity. Don't fail to scale, but ensure your new growth doesn't cause your loyal clients to suffer because of new acquisitions.

The automotive industry really doesn't get this principle. They function from a "now is better than tomorrow, and I really could care less about yesterday" as well mentality. Even though we preach, "There's fortune in the follow-up," we are only going to follow-up where we think there's fortune right now.

I've seen, too often, we through away what seems to not be ready for what seems to be ready, and then when it doesn't work out the way you thought, we find out that not-so-ready was actually more ready than what seemed to be a sure deal. With proper routines and regimen, both clients could've received the assistance they needed and deserved. Lesson learned: don't neglect what you know is right, in order to shortcut and receive what you didn't work for. If it seems too good to be true, it normally is too good to be true. I am living hope that a creative, impulsive, I-can-make-it-work type of person can mind-SHIFT to become a scheduled, routine operating individual. Ok! I'll never look as good as the assistant of the president, but I can learn how to live based upon a schedule and calendar.

My day is scheduled, and this is new for me. I've always had a great memory. I thought I could and would always function from my memory; I thought I would always just know what I needed to do and where I needed to be. This works when you're running a small business or only have a few commitment areas. When it's all about you and you only, I have another challenge for you. I made the adjustment in this arena when my Executive Coach, Lisa Nichols, challenged me to grow the business from day one to sale, even if I decided to buy it back from myself.

People don't buy what's in your head. They want to see it on paper. They want to know where it's been and what it has the potential to become. This must go beyond your great ability to communicate about it; this must be seen in the detailed organized documentation both of what has been done, as well as the projections of what will be done in the future. You see, they may hire me as their coach if I can deliver what I promise, but I limit my income potential and impact when things remain only within. Every quote given, I have to call; every e-mail sent, I have to send; and, every speech delivered, I have to give. There's only so much 'I' can do until I reach capacity. Oh, maybe I should've put this chapter earlier in the book, but for those who enjoy reading, you're getting the gold. We must find a way to duplicate, and then multiply our efforts if we are desiring the maximization R.O.I.

You may only know R.O.I. to be the Return on Investment. We, of course, need a return on our investment if we are going to call ourselves a business.

Without it we may need to see if we qualify for nonprofit status. Why do all the work that a business requires if you don't plan to make a profit? Someone might say, "You sure are talking a lot about the business model for your coaching firm. Are you not fearful of your clients hearing you speak about making a profit?"

I almost laughed, but we may not know each other well enough for that. To silence any doubts and to answer your question, "No, I'm not fearful. Matter-of-fact, if they're the right client, they have the expectation that I'm profitable and successful. How am I to help any of them through these crazy times, if I can't navigate the seas myself?" Now, it's not to say that I don't have clients who make more than my business, or I must prove my value in every area by experiencing first-hand the lessons I teach. I am simply saying we don't avoid words like success, profit, or market share to name a few.

The second and third definitions of R.O.I. that don't get discussed as much are: Return on Ideas and Return on Influence. These two areas of R.O.I. are what help us to multiply. John Maxwell dedicated his entire life to learning, teaching, and modeling how to exercise these principles for maximum production and profits. When you grow people, you begin tapping into unlimited resources and possibilities. You do realize that every handshake and hello is an opportunity to say, "Hello," to my dream and, "Good-bye," to my struggle, right?

Preneurs live for the opportunity. It doesn't matter if you're an Entrepreneur, Solopreneur, Mompreneur, Godpreneur, Dadpreneur, Authorpreneur, or Didn't Knowpreneur, there is an unlimited opportunity when we begin to invest in the lives of people. The Return on Influence is seen when I can't, but you can... When I don't know the person, but you have them on speed dial.

The last Live experience I did is a great example of a Return on Influence. My budget was tight. What I spent on Monday morning, I needed to close some deals on Monday afternoon in order to be able to spend on Wednesday. You get the picture; it was tight. The tighter the budget, the more creative the creative must become.

Everything is energy and functions within a vibration. There's a currency and flow to wealth that once we tap into, we must remain. It's easier understood by saying, "Where there's vision, there will always be provision." When I lack provision, I must look at all three R.O.I.'s. (Return on Investment, Return on Influence, and Return on Ideas) My answer will lie within one of these.

With that being the case, I got on the phone and started talking about my vision, not my problem. Vision inspires; vision ignites; and, vision invites. Problems need solutions, whereas vision opens up the opportunity of possibility. In a matter of three days, I received commitments for payment for all of the items of my experience minus $455. I think I can handle that number right there. Or, at least when the money would be needed, I'd have it.

What happened? I cast vision, and my business partners and friends heard inspiration. They were ignited to use their power, ability, and resources on my behalf. Oh, and yes, they also knew when I gave them the invitation to assist me to win, I needed their assistance. Don't miss this point here: When you add value, you become valuable. Investors are always looking to invest in people, places, and projects that are either valuable or add value. Free business is never free in my opinion; it's the unspoken yes you received with a deferred payment option.

Where I experienced the greatest teachings on faith was from a man in Houston named I.V. Hilliard. He would always say, "When you need it, you will have it. If you don't have it, you just don't need it yet. God will give you more along the way than He'll give you when you start." So, what you have is enough to get started. I started Assist U2 Win with a pen, a pad, and a plan.

I struggled with capacity limits because, early on, I operated my business from a poverty mindset. I'm not sure why I adopted this mindset, but I do know where it came from. My mindset was not because of my upbringing. My parents were in the military, and we always had more than enough. Not Fresh Prince of Bel-Air more, but enough to pay all the bills, go out to eat, and enjoy family vacations.

Looking back from the lens of an adult, I appreciate this because everybody doesn't get this luxury.

Unfortunately, we must maintain what we've been given, or we'll attach to what's not good for us. I know I am going into extra detail, but I feel the person who's reading this section is in need of a breakthrough, and I'm obligated to speak directly to you. My poverty mindset was birthed in my need to please people. I said it. Whew! Now that I've identified it, let me explain.

I had a limiting belief that was subtle and strong that said, "If they knew all about me, they wouldn't accept me." My tribe reading my book just said, "YANA" (You Are Not Alone). For the individual whose grabbing your tissue, know that I feel you. Let's slow down and deal with this devil, so we can go to the next level together.

I repeat from previous chapters, *I didn't love myself.* "But," you may be thinking, "You're successful." It doesn't matter; I didn't value my purpose. I only valued wanting to be popular. I didn't function from a pure heart. It only seemed like it because I was smooth. I had a problem with me that rooted back to my birth.

Listen, when you could've been labeled as an "oops," which I thought I was because I am 10 years younger than my sister and brother, it starts these feelings of am I supposed to be here. I also couldn't stand the skin I was in. I am a dark-skinned man, living in a world where the lighter the righter. In addition, I stuttered so badly that I was pulled from my class to work on my speech. Then, to add fuel to an already blazing fire, I had a gap that was larger than Michael Strahan's with a last name of Butts. No; bullying wasn't like it is today, but I still got my fair share. This feeling was cemented when I would make mistakes that found their way in confronting situations. I was a runner. I only wanted to be in situations where the accolades and cheers were screaming my name. I didn't want to deal with being human and real. I only wanted you to see my shine, always avoiding my mud.

We often hide in times like these and run from people or places that make you face you, the real you. The church and my faulty relationship with God had me believing that those who sin are doomed and will never be given or experience the words forgiveness, love, grace, and mercy. I allowed words like guilt, shame, condemnation, and grudge-holding to produce this unhealthy version of dodging and running when the heat got turned on. It was here where I realized that I lowered my value at the end of every mistake I encountered. So, the more mistakes, the lesser my value was to me, and in life that's what really matters.

Henry Ford said this, "Whether you think you can, or you think you can't, you're right." My thoughts about me were very low, and I didn't even know it until I started having to price my services. When everyone who really knew me would come around me, the first thing they would say is, "Why are your prices so low?" Here it is: value shows up in what you settle for.

Value shows in what you've identified your potential to now be. You once had high expectations, and now you just want to do okay. If you don't deal with the personality space of your life, it will hinder the production and projections that you believe are possible for your life. My good friend, Johnny Collins, says, "Don't let your lack of stop your in spite of." This statement is cute and nice to say, but when one really dives in and focuses on what he's saying, there are many, many breakthroughs one can experience.

It was in San Diego where I was led through a series of exercises that exposed my area of pain that was neatly put together and, when untouched, it didn't bother anyone. We learn to live with our limp. This is just gonna be my fate mentality, even though it's not what we desire nor what we dream. We learn to quiet our dream and tell it, "Not right now." The other fault we make is when we measure the wrong metrics. Metrics are milestone markers that can determine if we are winning or losing (actually opportunities for learning). Too many are winning under the wrong metrics, and they're not sure where they stand in the game we should be playing.

The programs I first offered were a lot of time given for a low investment level. To the outsider looking in, you're probably saying, this is what we call a great deal, and in some cases you're right. But in my case, it was attempting to serve everyone without offering a full menu. One size fits all is not what coaching is all about. Coaching is about customization and individual objectives, but I was trying to become all things to everyone hoping to gain someone—a bad, bad, and I mean bad methodology, which stemmed from a bad, bad, very bad mindset.

What areas of your life are you functioning beneath your potential and possibility? Is it working at the same place because you don't want to have someone turn down your resume? Are you not applying because they said... Wait, hold up. Who are the "they's saying" anyways? I'm telling you, enough is enough.

The last I checked, you are an original. You have your own thoughts, your own feelings, and your own set of standards that should make you happy. You need to hear it again, so I have to say it, "You build what you birth." I want you to birth your I Told You Statement. Now, before you finalize it, it must be ***bold, intentional, and unapologetic.*** Your I Told You Statement needs to give courage in the midst of fearful situations, strength to say no when you know you're expected to say yes, and the ability to fight through when life tries to block and stop you. This statement needs to focus your energy when the shiny distractions come to get you off course. This statement needs to be dripped in your inner-winner's attitude sauce, which can be used as fuel for your fire. It should echo to your hater, I *told* you, echo to your past, I *told* you, and echo to your future you, I *told* you.

So, the lightbulb came on for me after listening to Joel Ervay breakdown the 3% method for delivering a webinar. Now, I'm not going to attempt to write the method. Look him up, or watch a session. For now, just understand this thought: the rich purchase programs for results given in a short amount of time spent invested, while the poor value how much time you can offer and how low the pricing is advertised. So, if I spend all my time in your program, when am I going to have time to get into action? The rich say, "Show me what needs to be done in a concise, clear way, and I'll be ready to conquer through implementation." The flip side is also true; one buys for time to feel good without accountability to do well. As long as I feel like I'm making progress, and you keep giving me new information, then I value the course I paid for.

When this light bulb came on, I immediately implemented it. I had to be willing to let go of some clients in order to obtain my ideal client. Sometimes, your scale is in alignment and not in obtaining additional assignments. The only kids in school who needed to do extra work were the ones who didn't the work effectively the first time. When the audience I was serving became the audience I wasn't called to, I had to do too much to receive too little. My family suffered, my finances suffered, and my faith was challenged. I think I've emphasized over and over throughout this book that it's more in your systems than in your talent.

I've always been a talented speaker. I've always had the ability to assist people. But, I hadn't always had the ability to command the attention of a room, and then have the room want to invest their hard-earned money to join my community because of the results that were delivered time and time for those before them. Where are we in my schedule?

By noon, we've touched a minimum of four clients and, depending on the day, we're now looking over our "One Thing" List for the day. Oh, if I didn't mention it, this One Thing List is also done in my early waking time of the morning. Once I've finished coaching my morning clients, I now take a break, grab a bite to eat, and then dive into my one thing. My one thing could range anywhere from sending out 25 e-mails to companies, speaking agencies, or following up with e-mails from requests and proposals to preparing content for new talks, writing additional material, or recording videos for my communities. The point you need to see in this is my one thing is not just from my inspired mind, it is scheduled based on the desired results I want to achieve.

You don't replace a $250,000 salary just by going live on Facebook every day. You don't scale to a million-dollar business within 24 months because of t-shirts and a #1 Amazon best-seller. You have to bring much more focus and strategy when your wife has braces, your son is in college, and the bills that were easy to pay still come in without giving you a break to stabilize your newfound business. Assist U2 Win is tattooed on my left arm, so I wake seeing my why and my what. The napkin that holds my reason for leaving AutoNation is seen daily as I enter my home office. Shoot! I almost forgot, and I can't leave this out... This business started when I was working six days a week, 10-12-hour days.

Yes; I had to insert this right here because I felt someone saying, "If I was working full-time for myself, I definitely could do all of these things." I agree. It starts with what you have, where you are, and you build what you birth. When the baby that you feed grows larger than the crib, you have to buy the baby a new bed, or you'll soon stunt the growth of the child. Grow your baby and keep buying new beds along the way. If your desire is for full-time status with your dream, then it's possible. I won't tell you when to jump, but please know there's gonna come a time when you're just gonna have to jump. Jump because you want to. Jump because you have to. You're gonna have to jump, and when it's time just know you can't land until you leave.

You'll never land on the next level until you've decided to leave the level, you're on. It's been good, but you need to say, "Asta le vista, Baby." Find someone who admires you and begin mentoring them to take over the business that once was desirable and is now no longer yours.

LIVE COACHING AND TRAININGS (SCHEDULED)

Tuesdays and Thursdays are my live coaching and training days. If possible, I only schedule my consistent coaching clients on these days. I've built my business to function around my schedule. The reason for this is because I travel on the weekends, and many times Mondays and Fridays are travel days. Also, conferences and training workshops are often desired between Fridays and Mondays.

When I'm home, I do my best to keep my Mondays and Fridays open beyond coaching calls in the morning. These days are allotted to spending time with my family. Soon, I'm going to become an avid golfer again, but we can't pick this habit back up until we reach our *2020 I Told You* goals. If you haven't heard about *2020 I Told You*, this is our national movement that challenges each individual to form a bold, intentional, unapologetic statement that will change our community, city, and life.

MY EVENING TIME

If you ever want to see me slow down, please come to my house around 7:00 or 8:00 pm. I feel that I've run out of words, and my energy is at an all-time low. I've given my best all day, and right now I'm winding down. I'm tired! I do my best not to plan any meetings or calls in the evenings, unless it's a Thursday night. The evenings are reserved for non-producing outings that bring me a reward over a return. This could be watching Sariyah cheer, watching Torin play baseball, or attending a local high school basketball game. I would love to see Zion run, but he's in Houston, and his events are seasonal. Don't get me wrong, the wife and I love to travel to Zion's track meets and see Houston (#speedcity) compete against other track and field athletes. But, we can't make them all.

Friday night is also date night. From the moment Tamara and I started dating, we established our dating night. You had to do this being that my industry was so unpredictable, and my relationship was so fragile. When you're gone more than you're home, you must be intentional, relational, and purposeful with every intention. One of the primary reasons I left AutoNation to start Assist U2 Win was the desire to build freedom and then wealth. I didn't assume a lack of focus in a particular area resulted in poor outcomes; instead, I would give my best, guard my attitude, and daily show up giving my best to each task I was responsible for. Even as I'm writing, I'm winding down thinking about the backend of my day. This is not my time to shine, and I endure until the morning.

IT'S MY TIME TO SLEEP

Before retiring for the evening, I normally enjoy a talk with my wife. She and I recap our days, and then we'll just lay in bed messing on our phones. I've turned into a social swiper, while she enjoys playing word games on her Apple iPhone. Now, all of this is happening while we both watch our favorite channel, Discovery ID.

I must admit, I got addicted to certain shows with my favorite being Detective Joe Kenda. I normally fall asleep before everyone in the house, and if it gets quiet the whole house would know that I'm asleep. Yes; I snore. At least that's what I'm told. The only person who can endure my snoring is Sariyah. I think it's because growing up, Sariyah would fall asleep in my arms, and I must imagine she just got used to the sounds of *DJ Sleep Real Hard*.

And this completes my day. As you can see, the combination of a winning mindset—mixed with strategic methods—is the secret sauce that leads to dominant mastery. And, in conclusion of this book, I've included my 10 Rules of Winsday just for you!

THE END

You've made it to the end, and you're now ready to begin. I totally understand the feeling. If you're anything like me, you have some underlined quotes, adopted some new thoughts, and possibly you're wanting to learn more about me or my story. If that's the case, I want to invite you to a Complimentary Masterclass that I host once a month. If you're interested in learning more about this Masterclass, please visit: www.makeverydayawinsday.com

Once you register for this Masterclass, I want you to make it a point to schedule, so you don't miss it. During this Masterclass, depending on when you've read this book or when you attend, I will be teaching a lesson from *Make Every Day a Winsday* in a Coaching Style Format. Now, from time-to-time the class is full, and when this happens, we'll either open another class that month, or you will be put into the next one. Either way, you'll be notified, so you can plan your schedule accordingly. I'd be very honored if you would attend. Again, it's complimentary, and if you enjoyed the book, then you'll definitely enjoy our live class.

Finally, many of you are already following us on social media; however, if you haven't done so just yet, please know you have a personal invitation from me to do so. We have a very strong presence and a pretty active following on Facebook and Linkedin, so join us and help us keep the conversation going!

Thank you for taking the time to read my book, and I look forward to an Intentional Intersection at some point in our lives. For booking or coaching interests, please reach out to admin@assistu2win.com. Now, go and *Make Every Day a Winsday!*

ABOUT THE AUTHOR

A master motivator, communicator, and influencer, Derrick Butts is the CEO of Assist U2 Win: The Connecting Place for Winners. Derrick is known for his unique ability to communicate and to connect with his audience. He offers tons of value by sharing proven principles that create momentum, change, and strategy.

For 15 years Derrick has influenced thousands of lives to discover their definition of winning, to develop a plan and make it a reality, and to decide that *now* is greater than later to implement a plan for winning.

Derrick has 20 years of intense leadership training, combined with 15 years of leading highly successful sales and finance teams within AutoNation, and has been certified and coached by John Maxwell and company. He now spends his time investing in and imparting these proven principles into the lives of individuals and businesses.

One of today's newest innovative thought-provoking leaders, Derrick believes there are simple solutions to maximize personal development, production, and profits. For this he is sought after by many to inspire, to challenge, and to deliver winning principles to individuals, entrepreneurs, educators, and business leaders around the world. Derrick's love and passion is experienced when he ignites the winner within you to believe that you too can win. This is what he calls Assist U2 Win.

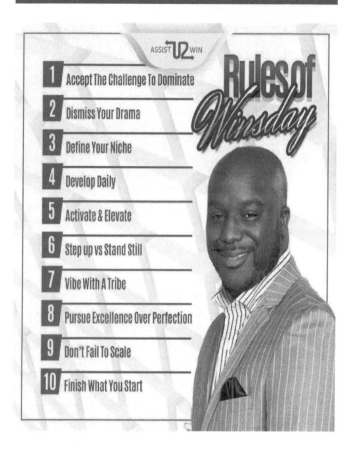

ASSIST U2 WIN

Rules of Winsday

1 Accept The Challenge To Dominate

2 Dismiss Your Drama

3 Define Your Niche

4 Develop Daily

5 Activate & Elevate

6 Step up vs Stand Still

7 Vibe With A Tribe

8 Pursue Excellence Over Perfection

9 Don't Fail To Scale

10 Finish What You Start